DATABASE MARKETING

DATABASE MARKETING
Strategy and Implementation

78318

Robert Shaw and Merlin Stone

WILEY

John Wiley & Sons
New York • Chichester • Brisbane • Toronto • Singapore

Published in Great Britain by Gower Publishing Company Limited
Published in North America by John Wiley and Sons, Inc.

Library of Congress Cataloging in Publication Data:

Shaw, Robert.
    Database marketing : strategy and implementation / Robert Shaw and
    Merlin Stone.
        p.   cm.
    Includes bibliographical references.
    ISBN 0-471-62345-8
    1. Marketing—Data bases. 2. Data base management. I. Stone,
    Merlin, 1948–   . II. Title.
    HF5415.125.S48   1988
    658.8′0028′5574—dc20   89-16598
                                                                        CIP

Printed in the United States of America

90 91 10 9 8 7 6 5 4 3 2 1

Preface

This book explains what database marketing is, what it can do and how a company can go about implementing it. Although many of the marketing and computing techniques which database marketing uses are well established, their combination into an all-embracing way of doing business is still relatively uncommon. This book aims to explain why marketing and corporate management should take a closer look at what database marketing has to offer.

This is not a detailed textbook. It has been written for managers who are in a position to influence significantly how their companies do their marketing (and of course for those who hope to be in that position in the future—whether less senior managers or students of marketing). We have aimed to provide a comprehensive overview of the whole topic in as short a space as possible. However, while we have not shied away from technical issues where we believe they should be discussed, the focus of the book is very clearly managerial.

The book is relevant to any company, of any size, in any industry, because any company can improve its relationship with its customers by implementing the approaches described in this book. The larger the company, or the wider its product range, or the more numerous its customers, or the more complex the distribution channels through which it works, the more challenging it will be to implement database marketing. But the pay-off will be greater!

Robert Shaw
Merlin Stone

Acknowledgments

This book is the result of many years of exciting and fruitful work. We have worked with and been helped by so many people that it would be impossible to name them all. So we thank all our friends, colleagues and clients for their help and encouragement, and hope that this book helps them in return, by providing a long overdue synthesis. However, there are three people we must mention by name.

Working on a variety of projects with Bob and Kate Kestnbaum, who lead the world in database marketing innovation, has stretched and stimulated our thinking while we were writing this book. Without them, many database marketing projects would have never seen the light of day. We feel honoured to be working with them.

Mike Wallbridge, as friend and client, continues to take us into new areas as he challenges the companies in which he works to take up the opportunities (and to go through the difficulties) involved in implementing database marketing. His vision, pace and dynamism often leave us gasping for air.

Robert Shaw
Merlin Stone

Contents

Figures

Part I
STRATEGIES AND PRINCIPLES

1 Introduction

In this book we explain:

- What database marketing is
- Why database marketing is growing so fast
- Who uses it and why
- What distinguishes it from more 'traditional' approaches to marketing
- How developments in technology have fuelled its growth
- What are the typical phases in its development
- What competitive advantages it offers
- How to use it by managing resources effectively and developing the right applications
- How to implement and manage it

What is database marketing?

There is no universally accepted definition of database marketing. In this book, we use the following definition:

Database marketing is an interactive approach to marketing, which uses individually addressable marketing media and channels (such as mail, telephone, and the sales force):

- To extend help to a company's target audience
- To stimulate their demand
- To stay close to them by recording and keeping an electronic database memory of customer, prospect and all communication and commercial

3

contacts, to help improve all future contacts and to ensure more realistic planning of all marketing.

Database marketing is a new, powerful approach to marketing for large companies. Many companies are spending large budgets on it. They include telecommunications, computer and office equipment suppliers such as AT&T, IBM and Xerox, automotive suppliers such as Ford and Volvo, and financial sector companies, such as banks and insurance companies. Ten years ago, these companies and many like them had barely considered how database marketing could work for them. Today they use various terms to refer to their version of database marketing, such as direct response, telemarketing, direct marketing, transactional advertising, mail order and curriculum marketing. But these terms refer to one or more of the many techniques used by database marketers. In this book, we use 'database marketing' to mean a new way of doing business, a re-definition of marketing management which leads to a new way of defining the relationship between a company and its customers.

Database marketing works by creating a bank of information about individual customers (e.g. taken from orders, enquiries, external lists), using it to analyse their buying and enquiry patterns, and thereby creating the ability to target products and services more accurately towards specific customers. For example, it may be used to promote the benefits of brand loyalty to customers at risk from competition. It can fuel revenue growth by identifying which customers are most likely to buy new products and services. It can increase sales effectiveness. It can support low cost alternatives to traditional sales methods. These include telemarketing and direct mail, which can be of strategic importance in markets where margins are being eroded.

By extending more coordinated forms of help to customers, through use of a unitary marketing database, and by measuring customers' responses to promotional campaigns, database marketing makes the marketing function more accountable for its results. By sharing marketing information and using it to promote corporate and brand image, it offers a way of improving the link between advertising and sales promotion, product management and sales channels. By closing the gap between various elements of the sales process, it reduces the likelihood of the customer being neglected.

The characteristics of database marketing are listed below and illustrated in Figure 1.1. However, companies come to database marketing in different ways, so not all these characteristics are visible in all companies which use it. The characteristics of fully fledged database marketing are:

1. Each actual or potential customer is identified as a record on the marketing database. Markets and market segments are not identified primarily through aggregate data, which cannot be broken down into individual customers, but as agglomerations of individual customers.
2. Each customer record contains not only identification and access information (e.g. name, address, telephone number), but also a range of

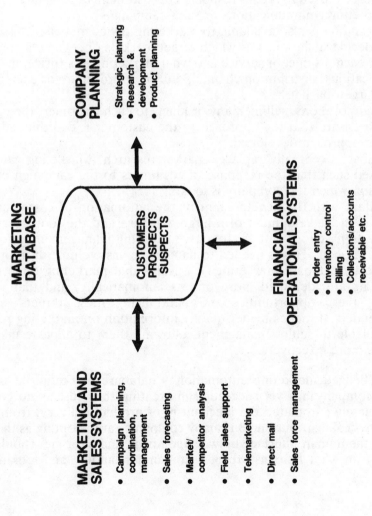

MARKETING DATABASE

CUSTOMERS
PROSPECTS
SUSPECTS

COMPANY PLANNING

- Strategic planning
- Research & development
- Product planning

MARKETING AND SALES SYSTEMS

- Campaign planning, coordination, management
- Sales forecasting
- Market/competitor analysis
- Field sales support
- Telemarketing
- Direct mail
- Sales force management

FINANCIAL AND OPERATIONAL SYSTEMS

- Order entry
- Inventory control
- Billing
- Collections/accounts receivable etc.

Figure 1.1: Fully integrated database marketing

marketing information. This includes information about customer needs and characteristics (demographic and psychographic information about consumers, industry type and decision making unit information for industrial customers). Such information is used to identify likely purchasers of particular products and how they should be approached. Each customer record also includes information about campaign communications (whether the customer has been exposed to particular marketing communications campaigns), about customer's past responses to communications which form part of the campaigns, and about past transactions (with the company and possibly with competitors).

3. The information is available to the company during the process of each communication with the customer, to enable it to decide how to respond to the customer's needs.

4. The database is used to record responses of customers to company initiatives (e.g. marketing communications or sales campaigns).

5. The information is also available to marketing policy makers. This enables them to decide such points as which target markets or segments are appropriate for each product or service and what marketing mix (price, marketing communications, distribution channel, etc.) is appropriate for each product in each target market.

6. In large corporations, selling many products to each customer, the database is used to ensure that the approach to the customer is coordinated, and a consistent approach developed.

7. The database eventually replaces market research. Marketing campaigns are devised such that the response of customers to the campaign provides information which the company is looking for.

8. Concomitant with the development of the automation of customer information via the development of a large database and the tools to access it to handle transactions with customers, marketing management automation is also developed. This is needed to handle the vast volume of information generated by database marketing. It ensures that marketing opportunities and threats are identified more or less automatically, and that ways of capturing these opportunities and neutralizing these threats are also recommended. It makes higher quality information on marketing performance available to senior managment, allowing them to allocate marketing resources more effectively.

This is fully fledged marketing automation – database marketing at its most mature. No company has yet succeeded in creating this, just as no company has yet completely automated the mechanism of product delivery, from design through to physical distribution. But many companies are adopting as their goal the idea that the human interface between company and customer should focus most strongly on what humans are best at – understanding and looking after each other.

For example, face-to-face sales staff may be best used in presenting difficult or radically new concepts to customers, or handling sensitive problems. Telemarketing staff may be best used in handling other sales tasks, such as managing smaller accounts, obtaining basic data needed to establish whether a prospect is a serious one, or identifying some of the facts relating to a sales problem. Both kinds of staff can concentrate more on exploiting their relative advantage if they are given the support of a powerful database marketing system. For this reason, database marketing is appearing in the strategic plans of many companies.

Why is database marketing growing so fast?

The very existence of database marketing is owed to the powerful processing capability and immense storage capacity of today's computers, and to the way telecommunications technology is being harnessed to make customer and market data available to the wide variety of staff involved in a company's marketing and sales efforts. Yet technology alone cannot explain the fast growth of database marketing.

Evidence of its rapid growth comes from various sources:

- In the US, over half of all advertising now asks for a direct response.
- In the UK, expenditure on direct mail is growing at over 30 per cent p.a. in real terms. This is much faster than expenditure on television.
- Almost every day, a new name is added to the list of large companies that have successfully added direct marketing to their communications strategy. In the US, users range from capital equipment companies to companies marketing low budget consumer goods and services. Retailers and mail order companies have been joined by the manufacturers of fast moving consumer goods. In the UK the already explosive growth in its use by the financial sector is likely to be further stimulated by continuing liberalization. Large retailers, chary of marketing disciplines which have developed out of branded goods marketing, are appointing direct marketing agencies. They are starting to exploit one of their chief assets – the database of loyal customers who hold their credit cards.
- Telemarketing capacity in the UK is doubling annually, whilst in the US the telephone is now the biggest single marketing medium.

This growth of database marketing is rooted in the philosophy of small businesses – a philosophy of getting closer to the customer. Many gurus of marketing and business thought preach the virtues of this philosophy. Identify your customers, understand their needs, meet these needs, treat your customers well after the sale, and you have a head start on your competitors.

All this is easily said, but less easy for large companies to put into practice. Much corporate marketing is still tied to big, general marketing campaigns that have a single message for everyone. Corporate marketing is dominated by the idea that it is the USP – the Unique Selling Proposition – that creates differentiation in the market place. In theory, the USP can be translated into one set of words and pictures which will guide all consumers to make the 'right' choice.

Developments in markets and technology are forcing large companies to question the idea of the market-wide USP. Instead, they are trying to put the small business philosophy into practice. Single USPs, spelt out to the whole market, are no longer enough. Customers can be helped to select from a wide variety of goods. But customers differ. They need different kinds of help and service. This can be provided by sending special messages tailored to specific segments of the market and sometimes to the market segment of one, the individual customer. This is the goal of database marketing, which aims to displace the overall USP approach, and make it seem increasingly a weak lowest common denominator in terms of its power to sell.

Computerizing information about customers and their relationship with us makes it possible to address help and service more specifically. It can also be used to market a variety of additional goods and services to each customer. This combination of satisfying customer needs for more information and marketing to the customer at the same time is the main competitive advantage of database marketing. It provides the main motive for companies to invest in it. But all this would be impossible without enabling developments in technology.

The strengths of database marketing

Why do we use database marketing in preference to other approaches? Database marketing has special strengths.

- It is *measurable*. Responses to campaigns are measured, enabling us to identify the effectiveness of different approaches.
- It is *testable*. We can test the effectiveness of different elements of our approach – the product, the communications medium, the offer (how the product is packaged to appeal to the customer), the target market, and so on. Tests can be carried out quickly, so we can take quick action on the results. We can use test campaign results to forecast sales more precisely, helping us to manage inventory more effectively.
- It is *selective*. We can focus campaigns accurately, because we communicate with specific customers.
- We can *personalize* communication to each customer, by including details relevant to them and not to others. This usually raises the response rate.
- It is *flexible* – we can time our campaigns to have their effect exactly when we want.

There are other reasons why the use of database marketing is growing so quickly. What were thought to be mass markets are splitting into new, distinct buying segments. In consumer markets, rising incomes are allowing people to indulge tastes for more discretionary goods. In business markets, buyers are becoming more expert, seeking information about products from a wider variety of sources and expecting to have their needs met more precisely than before. Suppliers' ability to analyse customer needs has increased with the use of new techniques and lower costs in market research, so niche marketing by suppliers has helped to fragment markets.

The costs of mass marketing have risen. Television costs continue to rise rapidly relative to the costs of a mail shot, a sales call or a telephone call. But the costs of unstructured use of sales staff have also risen. Using advances in computing, telecommunications and print technology, more precisely targeted media – the 'narrowcast' media – are now available to cater for suppliers' needs to access particular market segments and for customers to receive information more relevant to their needs.

Developments in technology

In many respects, the computerization of businesses is at an early stage. Enabling technologies are developing fast. Most technologies, such as those which determine processing power and speed, memory and storage, are improving at least tenfold every ten years. Speed of access (reading, writing) to stored data is growing more slowly (about 5 per cent faster each year). Communications technology, once slow to evolve, is accelerating. Software, once a barrier, is now easier to use and more reliable. Mainframe and decision support packages are widely used for large modelling exercises and developing departmental administrative systems. Application packages are more functional and flexible and capable of customization. Application development products have accelerated programmer productivity. End-user computing has created experience and even expertise in handling computers throughout organizations.

The implications of these developments are:

1. Computerization of more difficult areas (e.g. marketing, because it covers people not controlled by the company – customers) is becoming easier. But no projects are easy. Large scale projects are always difficult. Creation of a very large customer-focused database is not to be undertaken lightly.
2. Large data-based systems will be used to drive customer communication and management, even in the most complex businesses.
3. Companies which do not plan their marketing data and management architectures will have difficulty in exploiting developments.

2 Users and suppliers

Database marketing usually grows out of the direct marketing function of an organization. This function has often been set up to carry out a specific, often tactical sales task, such as providing higher quality leads for the sales force, or managing an in-house credit card operation. But there are many potential users of database marketing outside the traditional direct marketing function. They include:

- Telemarketing operations, which may use the database marketing approach to manage some customers almost entirely by telephone.
- Field sales support, where the sales office may be the focus for all customer management, and the calling sales force is managed through the customer database rather than through the inclinations of local sales management.
- Customer service, particularly in companies marketing complex equipment, where the database is used as the key to managing the full range of pre- and post sales activity.
- Credit collection, where credit/debit status of the customer is used as a principal criterion for future relationships, adding an additional weapon to the credit collector's armoury.

Potential users by industry

Power and water utilities

The utilities satisfy some of the basic needs of consumers and organizations – heat, light, power and water. Public utilities are exploiting some of the marketing communications opportunities open to them. These range from 'bill-sweetening' stuffers explaining the nature and benefits of the service being provided, to appliance and maintenance service marketing, and 'piggy-back' mailings. The utilities benefit from strong coverage of potential markets – a powerful asset if additional data are added. However, they are often at an early stage in developing a marketing understanding of their customers. In some respects, the strength of the utilities as marketing entities derives from their regular billing arrangements. Pressure to allow more direct debiting and less frequent communication with customers may reduce the strength of their customer dialogue.

Financial sector

Companies in the financial sector provide ways for customers to manage their assets and liabilities (including cash), to achieve their desired income and expediture profiles over their lifetimes. The sector includes marketers of insurance, pensions, savings and credit, credit and charge cards, banking and mortgage services. It presents some of the greatest opportunities for database marketing. The underlying growth rate of this sector, relative to the economy, seems assured. Rising incomes (which generate larger absolute amounts of saving), increasing longevity and earlier retirement (and the need to fund a longer retirement), uncertain involvement of the state in providing for eventualities, and a (partly) supplier-stimulated awareness of the need for improved management of personal financial affairs are just some of the factors leading to this.

Coupled with these demand-side factors are supply-side factors, one of which is increasing competition as companies traditionally confined to one sector start to market other services, freed by liberalization of one kind or another to do so. This tendency is reinforced by the consequent higher marketing awareness within these companies. Rising staff and real estate costs have driven the search for different ways of managing relationships with customers other than through traditional agents and branches. These different ways are being made possible by the development of telecommunications and computing technology.

The sector is moving heavily into true database marketing. Many companies have accepted the principle of lifetime customer value as a relevant variable in the acquisition equation. This permits them to use more proactive marketing techniques to prospect, but this prospecting is sometimes limited to traditional product areas. As customers reveal more and more data about their needs, transactions and behaviour, it becomes possible to take a true database marketing approach, reappraising the relationship between the company and its customers for new opportunities, whether or not in financial services.

An application which eases this transition is the credit card or similar device. Looked at from the database marketing perspective, cards are no more than a customer identification technology, which happens to facilitate transactions and credit. Smart cards are an emerging addition to the technological portfolio.

Cards create postal and electronic traffic and hence opportunities of selling direct. More importantly, they also lead to the creation of a coherent picture of customer behaviour and needs, a prerequisite of true database marketing.

Leisure and travel services

The leisure and travel services sector includes all suppliers of personal transport (rail, air, coach, shipping, car hire, etc.), of accommodation (hotels, time-share, etc.), of packaged and tailor-made holidays, travel agents, motoring organizations, leisure operators (bingo, gambling clubs, betting shops, theme parks, and the like), photographic processors, theatres and cinemas, and publishers.

With so much information potentially (and actually, in some cases) available to suppliers concerning customer behaviour and preferences, the penetration of even primitive direct marketing into some areas of this sector (e.g. hotels) has been slow. This contrasts with other areas (e.g. airlines, certain holiday companies and cruise operators), where the value of a long term relationship with customers is well appreciated and exploited through a continuing dialogue. Here, too, marketing strategies are based on customer relationships (e.g. frequent flyer packages, special sea cruises for previous customers).

Given the long term robustness of this category of expenditure and (in some sectors, such as hotels, packaged holidays, car hire) the concentration of a high proportion of business in a few companies, the potential for database marketing is immense. In addition, from a tactical perspective, there are cross-selling opportunities within this sector. In some areas, distribution channel management and control issues (e.g. with travel agents) have slowed the progress of database marketing, by handicapping its economics (selling direct but taking bookings through agents), but this problem is expected to decline.

Some motoring organizations are so far along the marketing communications route that they have become mail order businesses. In the UK, the Automobile Association is now the largest direct sales organization for motor insurance. Many companies are involved in direct mail publishing. The success of the best of them derives from careful list extensions based on testing and statistical analysis of results.

Non-profit institutions

Political parties and charities will see a considerable widening of the use of database marketing, in recruiting members and influencing voting, through the maintenance of dialogue. Charities are heavy users of direct mail, and understand the characteristics of more generous givers, and also their tendency to give to several different charities – hence list exchanging between them. Trade unions are using database marketing techniques to organize elections. Some have introduced 'affinity group credit cards' as an additional service to their members. The marketing and administration of such cards relies heavily on database marketing techniques. Governments are considering ways of using database marketing techniques – whether in disseminating information, such as people's rights, or in tax collection.

Marketers of physical products

All physical product marketers have the following problems:

- The processes of manufacturing and physical distribution, which increase the time and costs involved in adjusting supply to demand
- The presence (in many cases) of retailers or distributors between the supplier and the customer, making their own merchandise selection and marketing policies. In the case of retailers, manufacturers have a major shared problem.

The divide between this sector and the previous ones is less and less obvious. Those mentioned earlier are increasingly working to classic marketing disciplines. They are packaging their products ever more professionally and make the long term commitments which enable them to do so (e.g. block bookings of hotels, construction of holiday facilities targeted at specific groups of customers). Product marketers are meanwhile beginning to understand the importance of creating a relationship over several purchases.

Products covered here include household durables, cars, home improvement products and fast moving consumer goods, such as food. In general, suppliers of these products have been slow to awaken to the opportunities of database marketing. One exception to this is the motor industry, which uses it to sustain dialogue after purchase, and for prospecting. Domestic appliance manufacturers have for long tussled with the question of how to maintain a cost-effective dialogue with customers when replacement for a given appliance is typically once every 7–10 years. They usually resort to retail display and occasional media bursts. Enhanced ability to segment and access particular groups of customers will help them solve this problem. However, they will still need to move away from a marketing communications emphasis to total database marketing if they are to be able to explore the full potential of their (usually multi-product) relationship with customers. For example, a typical household might have as many as 10 or 15 large and small appliances, many of which could have been sourced from one manufacturer. Some home improvement products are similar to appliances (e.g. DIY tools). Others, such as double glazing and kitchens, because of their close connection with a major life-time asset – the family home, have strong marketing parallels with financial services.

Fast moving consumer goods are a source of much controversy in database marketing circles. Some hold that the contribution of database marketing is bound to be limited. However, some families may well be spending hundreds of pounds a year on products from a given manufacturer. If cross-product branding is nurtured, these customers become good prospects for database marketing. Their lifetime value is certainly greater than that for many financial products. The potential competitive pay-off to successful database marketing in this area, where the only alternative is massive media spend, is clearly great.

Meanwhile, the tactical promotional use of database marketing is receiving more attention from companies in this sector. Many promotions currently being mounted are single product promotions which yield consumer lists as a by-product. Many are toll-free telephone campaigns. Here are some examples of incentives to call in (and to buy the product in the first place, of course):

- To find out if the consumer has won the prize described on the pack
- To answer questions on the product, receive a coupon and perhaps a prize
- To listen to a commercial, receive a coupon and a free gift
- To listen to a pop star's promotional message for a record

Retailers

The marketing problem of retailers is in a way a combination of those of the previous groups. For example, retailers are nearly utility companies for some consumers – a source of the basics – food and clothing. They play a very important part in financial transactions, representing the destination of most cash. Retailers are used at least as frequently as banks. They are providers of a service (halfway between leisure and work), but they are also product marketers in their own right.

The main difference between product marketers and multiple retailers is the sheer volume of data about customer needs that they can collect because of frequent and direct contact. This makes them prime candidates for database marketing.

Initially slow to take up marketing, let alone database marketing, most large retailers are rapidly developing their marketing resources and skills. This is partly as a result of the intense competitive pressure occurring in some sectors by mergers, take-overs, extension of product lines and regional extensions of operations. Retail management is now much more aware of the lifetime values of their customers and of how database marketing can provide ways of keeping customers. The retail credit card (and eventual full point of sale automation and smart cards) provides them with a strong weapon in their competitive armoury. Retailers already realize the tactical value of these techniques. But they need to understand their strategic value.

Mail order houses

Mail order houses are one of the largest users of direct mail. Their databases are now used for agent recruitment, promotions and also third party promotions. The use of specialized catalogues is becoming widespread. The question these companies must ask themselves is what their role will be when everyone else becomes a database marketer!

The demand for database marketing

For the foreseeable future, the trends encouraging the increased use of database marketing are likely to continue. Some of these factors relate to the markets in which database marketing users operate. They include the following:

- Increased fragmentation of consumer markets, partly as a result of more database marketing being used. This leads to increased ability on the part of suppliers to meet the needs of small groups of consumers, which puts pressure on non-users of database marketing to start using it, causing existing users to improve their use of it, and so on. In many consumer markets, companies will find it necessary not only to target their communications more precisely and manage their relationship with customers in a more 'personal' way, but also to plan their business using the ever more detailed information accumulated about their customers, and the ever more sophisticated tools available for them to do this planning.
- Fragmentation of business markets may also occur, for similar reasons. Other factors putting further pressure on industrial marketers to target their marketing more precisely include the steadily increasing professionalism and knowledge of industrial 'buying centres' (from professional buyers to users, influencers, etc) and the pressure that customers' managers are increasingly put under to make more effective use of their time and resources.
- In consumer and industrial markets, increased awareness of the absolute and competitive benefits of using computer and communications technology to manage customers. In many markets, companies are keeping a watchful eye on their competitors' attempts to implement particular facets of database marketing. This applies especially in its use for marketing planning, where developments are kept very close to the chest. In its use for marketing communications, secrecy is obviously more difficult.
- In all markets, increased emphasis on 'getting closer to the customer'. In the 1970s and 1980s, many supposedly marketing-oriented companies were chastened by their marketing experiences. Thinking that the information provided by relatively infrequent and superficial market research gave them good understanding of their customers, some companies were distressed to find that their customers' loyalty was much less than they supposed, or that they were wrong about the kind of customers they had.
- In many businesses, the presence of one of a small but increasing band of professionals with direct marketing or similar backgrounds. These managers are demanding that their companies examine and experiment with the best

that database marketing has to offer, not just in marketing communications, but in all marketing.

- In many public sector organizations, greater sensitivity to the needs of 'customers' (patients, users, consumers, ratepayers, etc.). This is emerging not only in the 'attitude' training being undertaken by many organizations, but also in the kinds of information technology being installed to give better service to 'customers'. Some of them are actively looking to improve communication with their 'customers'.
- In charities, political organizations and pressure groups, increased striving to influence people and reach them first and/or more effectively. Some charities are expert users of direct marketing. Here, the same competitive pressures apply as in consumer and industrial markets.

These trends spell radically increased opportunities for companies serving the database marketing market. The leading edge suppliers in this market form a new group of specialist companies, who work to turn the most advanced technology and marketing concepts into usable database marketing systems.

The supply of database marketing services

The 'supply-side' factors encouraging increased use of database marketing include:

- Further advances in computing and telecommunications. This makes it easier and cheaper to hold more complex information about individual customers or users. This information can then be analysed more comprehensively, accurately and quickly, and analyses can be integrated more immediately into policy. Relationships with customers can be managed more professionally, using the information held on the database or generated during each step in the relationship.
- Relative increases in the costs of other more labour or media intensive modes of marketing, and relative weakness in performance. In the US, the lack of national and often regional broadcast and printed media and the relative cheapness of classical direct marketing media (post and telephone) may have been factors in the dramatically higher usage of the latter for marketing purposes than in the UK. In the UK, the situation may never be the same, but the same trend is evident.

These developments offer greatly increased opportunities for the many suppliers who want to help businesses communicate with their markets. The suppliers staking their claims in this market include:

- Direct marketing and advertising agencies, many of whom have spawned direct marketing subsidiaries in recent years. Some are still being spawned.

- List brokers, who make their money helping prospective users tread their way through the minefield of prospective list suppliers.
- Database suppliers, who rent or sell their information, either as a complete database or in the form of a list. Many offer sophisticated selection and modelling services. Some offer ways of enhancing clients own lists.
- Database management and service agencies, who manage customer databases on behalf of their clients, or offer computing expertise specifically targeted at database marketing companies.
- Telemarketing agencies, who offer users their services in contacting prospective customers, or training their own people to do so.
- Mailing houses, who perform a similar service through the post, ranging from production of print through to mailing and follow-up.
- Print bureaux, who automate some elements of print and mailing.
- Other suppliers who help with individual elements of preparing a direct marketing package.
- Owners of proprietary lists who might be tempted into the market, possibly in combination with a database service agency.
- Owners of communications media (postal, telephone, publishing).

Many of these suppliers are broadening out the range of services supplied. With this rapidly developing supply of services, no company which needs to stay in touch with its customers has the excuse that it does not know how to use database marketing.

3 A strategic weapon

Some of the techniques characteristic of database marketing may be used by some companies solely as tactical weapons. For example, a direct response campaign may be aimed at a target market which proved difficult to access by other means. When used in this way, these techniques have much in common with other uses of customer data to achieve short term marketing goals. For example, the sales force of an industrial equipment company might be asked to analyse customers' records to find those with a particular product and encourage them to trade the product in for another product, or to purchase a maintenance contract.

However, the experience of many leading companies shows that database marketing is more effective when used strategically, to transform the way the company does business. Database marketing is a unique strategic weapon for achieving competitive advantage, as we show shortly. But if companies are to achieve maximum benefit from database marketing, their senior management must understand more clearly exactly how it can be used as a competitive weapon.

The adoption of full database marketing has many long term effects on business structure and culture. For example, the measurability of the results of database marketing makes the marketing function fully accountable for all its expenditure. The hard business results of their activities can be identified, traced back to the activities and the benefits set against the costs. This accountability is a positive one. Measurability makes it much easier to test the effectiveness of different approaches, giving the marketing function the tools to improve results. Database marketing therefore not only provides ways to control the marketing function, but also ways to improve performance.

However, this accountability creates great pressures within marketing. One reason for this is that in many companies, the marketing function is not truly accountable for all its policies. It may be accountable in a general sense, but the information may simply not be available to hold marketing accountable for particular policies. For example, the results of a change in promotional policy or in sales force compensation may not be accurately measurable. Database marketing changes this.

Pressures may also be created between marketing and other functions. This is because in some companies, many of the initiatives which marketing functions are asked to support come from other functions. In some types of company, these initiatives may come from engineering or product design. In others, they may come from finance or from a separate sales division. In other companies, they may even come from production ('we can make it, so you find ways of selling it', or, worse, 'we've got excess inventory, so find a way to sell it').

Without accountability for marketing expenditure, it is easy for each side to blame the other if, say, a new product fails. With a more disciplined and accountable approach, it will be quite clear where the blame lies. This may in turn change the relationship between marketing and other functions. They are both likely to want to work more closely together, using the database, in every area from product policy through to distribution.

The strategic role of database marketing

Database marketing is made possible by advances in information technology. Much of the understanding of the strategic role of information technology in general comes from work undertaken by Michael Porter at Harvard Business School. Professor Porter's work on this arose out of a wider programme of research into competitive analysis and strategy. As part of his analysis, Porter identified five competitive opportunity areas for information technology, as follows:

- Changing the basis of competition (CF1)
- Strengthening customer relationships (CF2)
- Overcoming supplier problems (CF3)
- Building barriers against new entrants (CF4)
- Generating new products (CF5)

The abbreviations in brackets refer to the competitive forces shown in Figure 3.1.

If a particular information technology approach can do any of the above, then it should be evaluated in terms of corporate strategy, and not be judged solely in terms of, say, the costs and benefits of particular ways of storing, processing and communicating information. We believe that for many companies, database marketing offers opportunities in all the above areas and

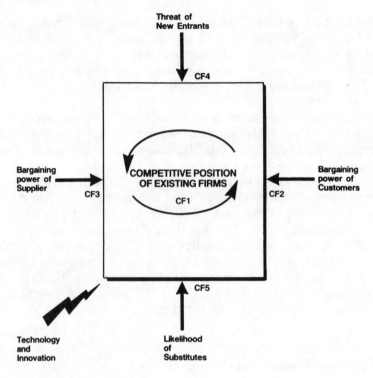

Figure 3.1: Competitive forces

therefore demands strategic evaluation. Let us look at these forces in more detail.

Competitive superiority

A business can establish a position of competitive superiority by building and exploiting a database with comprehensive coverage of its existing and potential customers for current and future products and services. Figure 3.2 shows how a company might plan to do this.

One of the most aggressive uses of the database would be to win customers from competition (conquest sales). For example, a leading US automobile manufacturer regularly attacks its competitors by using the automobile licence database (which covers all car owners) to target mail questionnaires at their competitors' customers. Typically, 20–30 per cent of these customers respond. Their responses provide valuable market research data. The data allow the company to identify, for example, those customers who are unhappy with their last purchase. These customers are then sent communications, tailored to each individual. The communication encourages them to consider the make supplied by the company. It also contains an incentive for them to take the first step in

COMPETITIVE SUPERIORITY THROUGH DATABASE MARKETING

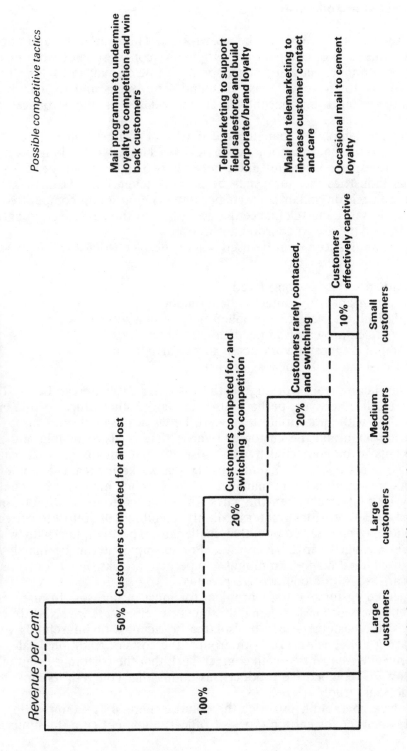

Revenue per cent

Possible competitive tactics

Mail programme to undermine loyalty to competition and win back customers

Telemarketing to support field salesforce and build corporate/brand loyalty

Mail and telemarketing to increase customer contact and care

Occasional mail to cement loyalty

Customers competed for and lost

Customers competed for, and switching to competition

Customers rarely contacted, and switching

Customers effectively captive

50%

20%

20%

10%

100%

Large customers

Large customers

Medium customers

Small customers

Figure 3.2: Achieving competitive superiority

that direction (e.g. a visit to the showroom). This marketing approach clearly changes the basis of competition. Originally, conquest sales were made solely by broadcast advertising and strong point of sale display and sales effort. Now, expertise in using the database to identify prospects and to 'narrowcast', by tailoring messages and incentives to individuals, is the strongest mode of competitive attack.

Another example of changing the nature of competition is where database marketing is used to transform how a field sales force works. In many industries, the field salesperson can only make between two and five calls per day (although in some industries the norm may be ten). A telemarketer can make between 20 and 50 decision maker contacts per day. The optimum competitive policy is to use field sales and telemarketing according to their relative strengths, using a customer database to coordinate the two.

Thus the sales force can be used where the face to face call is needed. This is likely to be where:

- Personal service is considered essential
- An important new contact is being made
- A difficult and sensitive problem needs to be solved
- A complex presentation needs to be made
- In-depth diagnostic work needs to be carried out
- The customer asks for a sales visit.

A telemarketing team working off the customer database can be used to cover all other call objectives, perhaps also calling on other offices of the customer. Eventually, with appropriate teamwork between the field sales force, the telemarketing team and the customer (whose time is also valuable and therefore who wants to be contacted by the most effective means for each call), more complex objectives can be handled by the telemarketing team. The telemarketer may become a full account manager. This approach increases the quantity and quality of contact between the sales force and customers, without increasing the cost. It also provides greater flexibility, enabling sales effort to be redeployed more quickly to meet competitive challenges. The discipline with which sales effort is managed can be increased. For example, it can be marshalled in a more disciplined manner to mount competitive attacks on customers known to be dissatisfied with a competitive product.

Neglected customers are a problem for most businesses. In many industrial product or service markets, small business customers are involved. In consumer markets, the customers may be isolated households or households with lower purchasing frequencies. For both groups, the costs of traditional sales channels may preclude frequent enough contact, such that the customer eventually gravitates towards competitive products, assuming that competitors have not fallen into the same trap!

Database marketing provides the solution here. For example, in the small business market for certain types of office equipment (e.g. facsimile, copiers, personal computers and telephones), the direct response advertisement and the catalogue, coordinated through the customer database, is becoming the industry standard for reaching the customer. Once the prospect has become a customer, database marketing can be used to maintain the dialogue, while supplies and upgrades are bought, until the equipment needs replacing.

Customer relationships

Database marketing can be used to improve a company's relationships with its customers, not only in acquiring them and defending them, but also in stimulating revenue growth.

Database marketing can be particularly effective in establishing the new customer relationships required to ensure the success of a new product launch. Typically, the product development function uses market research to determine the features, functions, applications, advantages and benefits required by customers. Research is also used to measure and segment the market. In many industrial markets, we know that the most successful innovations are those where potential customers were in close contact with the company from the earliest stage of product conception. Indeed, many successful innovations are actually made by customers!

In this case, rather than using market research to cover customers on a sample basis, database marketing can be used to contact many and possibly all potential customers for a product and create and sustain a dialogue with them from product conception through to launch.

Using both market research and database marketing can be very expensive. It can also lead to delays. Many companies involved in the personal computer market in its initial phases discovered this. They used market research to identify general needs, and then had to create prospect databases for direct response campaigns. They would have achieved more at lower cost had they built prospect databases from the beginning.

For existing products, database marketing provides an ideal way of building loyalty and maximizing revenue. For example, an automobile manufacturer regularly sends a questionnaire to all its customers. This monitors customer satisfaction and intentions to purchase. The results of the questionnaire are used to identify problems and ensure that dissatisfied customers do not become ex-customers. The results are also used to structure campaigns aimed at managing the replacement cycle. This ranges from providing messages to reinforce satisfaction to ensuring that the first step in replacement is the right one. For this, the normal contact programme involves two main mailings for the typical replacement cycle of three years. The first mailing is a few weeks after purchase, when the customer most needs to be reassured about the decision he has taken, The second is two years after the purchase, and is aimed at initiating a dialogue with the customer that will result in a sale by the end of the third year.

Alternative sales channels

Many businesses find that their ability to serve the growing and changing needs of their customers is constrained by the cost of accessing them – the cost of the sale. The supply of cost-effective skilled labour for selling and promoting sales and for servicing the customer after the sale is becoming increasingly scarce. Many businesses are turning to database marketing to solve this supply problem.

Database marketing can lower the cost of sales, through applications such as telemarketing, mail order, enquiry management, and the like. For example, an oil company made significant reductions in its field sales force by establishing a telemarketing team. In some industries, mail order has taken over many of the traditional functions of the sales representative e.g. the insurance industry. One large company has reduced the disruptive effect on local sales offices of pre-sales enquiries generated by national advertising, by directing these enquiries to a specialist customer information centre. Here, staff use scripted on-line customer prompts to gather the information needed to screen enquiries before sending out a sales representative. Pure literature gatherers and less interested customers are screened out and given other treatment, ensuring that they remain satisfied without incurring the cost of a sales call. In all these examples, the key to success is to match the cost of sales (channel cost) with the value of the customer. Figures 3.3 and 3.4 illustrate this point.

In some companies, whole product divisions are using database marketing as their main process for handling the sale. This applies to the 'supplies' (consumables and user-replaceable parts) divisions of many manufacturers of complex equipment.

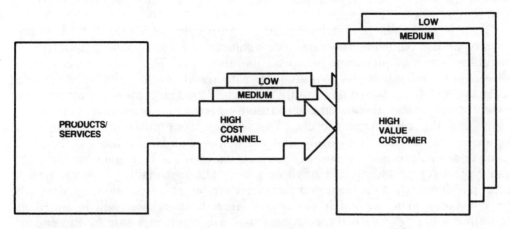

Figure 3.3: Channel cost matched to customer value

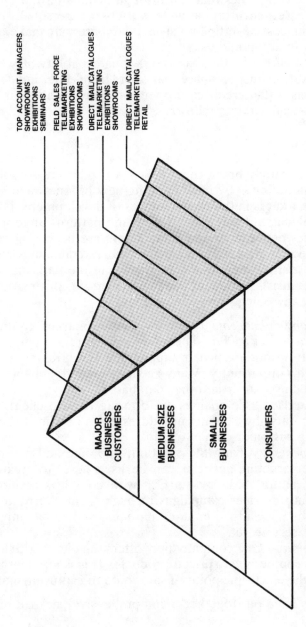

TOP ACCOUNT MANAGERS
SHOWROOMS
EXHIBITIONS
SEMINARS

FIELD SALES FORCE
TELEMARKETING
EXHIBITIONS
SHOWROOMS

DIRECT MAIL/CATALOGUES
TELEMARKETING
EXHIBITIONS
SHOWROOMS

DIRECT MAIL/CATALOGUES
TELEMARKETING
RETAIL

MAJOR
BUSINESS
CUSTOMERS

MEDIUM SIZE
BUSINESSES

SMALL
BUSINESSES

CONSUMERS

Figure 3.4: Best customers matched with best sales resources

Barriers to market entry

Businesses which do not possess a relevant marketing database may find themselves unable to enter a market, when faced with competitors who hold such a database and use it effectively. In some cases, this database can be a unique asset. For example, companies that sell through dealers have a unique asset in their dealer database, covering a wide variety of personal, financial and marketing data. The cost of setting up such a database may make entry difficult or impossible for other contenders.

Conversely, possession of a database marketing capability may be the key to entering new markets. Thus, database marketers from other industries (e.g. car owners' associations, retail credit card operators) have used their capability to break into the financial services industry.

New products and services

Information is increasingly being regarded as a product to be sold in its own right. Database marketing is by itself creating new products and services. This new information market is in the earliest stages of development. It is impossible to foresee the final shape it will take. But certain patterns are emerging.

Strategic alliances between database marketers are beginning to be formed. Banks, automobile manufacturers, financial services companies and publishers are planning new joint venture businesses, pooling the data that each possess to build a comprehensive picture of their customers. In this market, a number of services are already being provided, such as:

- *Data vending and enhancement*, already a major market. In the US, its size is already estimated at $500m. There, over 30,000 third party lists can now be purchased from one particular supplier. In the UK, many suppliers are waking up to this opportunity. Many agencies offer to enhance a company's database by adding data from other databases.
- *Data laundry services*. Companies are offering to help clients improve the quality of their data, by cleaning up addresses and adding other third party data to existing customer data.
- *Data management*, involving the creation, updating and maintenance of a database. Telemarketing agencies can be used here, to create a qualified customer information base by starting with cold lists, calling to qualify them, and managing sales campaigns through them. Currently the market is dominated by specialist computer bureaux, but few companies offer a comprehensive service yet.
- *Electronic shopping*. One company now offers the electronic shopper access to over 30,000 competitively priced products. This is a potentially powerful alternative to the electronic point of sale route to capturing marketing data.

Several companies have put together a comprehensive package of services for database marketers. Several offshoots of large mail order and retailing companies are offering the following kinds of service:

- Creative services
- Credit checking
- Credit card application handling, processing, and administration
- Data verification and management
- Data pooling between clients
- Data rental
- A comprehensive geodemographic consumer classification system
- Mail services
- Telemarketing
- Household distribution
- Statistical, analytical and consultancy services.

These are just some of the opportunities opened up by database marketing. The question is – how can we make it work? There are two kinds of answer to this: – the strategic and the operational. We must get both right. Without a clear view of our strategy, we will end up with a series of tactical programmes, some of which may be profitable in their own right. But they will lack the power to transform the way we do business and to create new sources of competitive advantage. Without well designed and managed operations, we may do the right things, but at costs which are prohibitively high and with results which do not justify the investment.

4 Choosing the right strategy

As the examples in the last chapter showed, companies in many industries can benefit from applying database marketing and other information technology developments to their relationships with customers. However, this proposition raises many questions. Two of the most important are:

- Can management tell whether a particular strategy is the right one?
- Is there a systematic way of identifying the right strategy?

We believe that the answer to these questions is yes. In this chapter, we outline how companies can identify the right strategy, and in particular:

- The guidelines which should be followed in assessing opportunities
- How to identify the most relevant opportunities
- The factors that should be taken into account in developing and delivering applications.

The approach we present here can be used by any organization which wants to identify opportunities for applying database marketing and pursue them quickly. The stages and tasks involved are depicted in Figure 4.1 together with the kinds of question addressed at each stage.

The innovative process

Applying database marketing is an innovative process. It is not a straightforward extension of existing ways of doing business. This process of innovation must be consciously initiated. This requires:

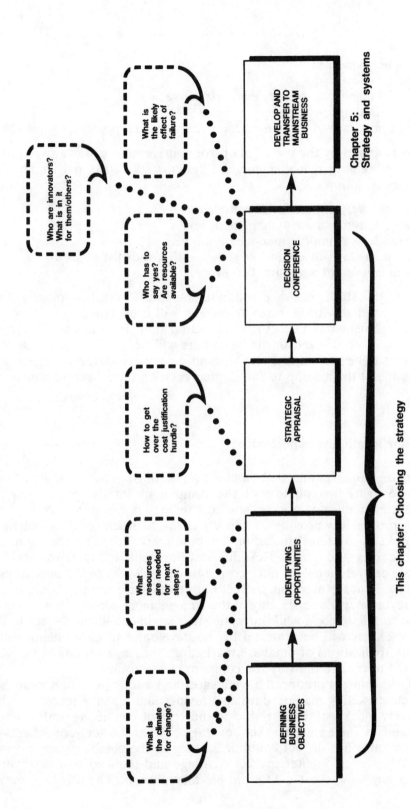

Figure 4.1: Choosing and implementing strategy

- Introducing managers to this new perspective
- Getting their support
- Creating a mechanism for generating and evaluating proposed applications.

The process is driven by the use of intensive management workshops, in which general and marketing management and systems specialists participate. The main steps are as follows:

1. Obtain top level support for the process
2. Generate ideas at senior management levels
3. Generate ideas at middle management levels
4. Develop plans for proceeding, together with a shortlist of ideas
5. Obtain management agreement to proceed.

At the end of this stage, resource commitments must be made. Initially, these commitments are likely to be small scale, and will consist mostly of feasibility studies. Management will need to be reassured that the impact of the applications on the company and on its customers will be professionally assessed. They will want to be certain that all the requirements (resources, changed ways of doing business) for moving to full implementation have been identified and analysed.

Guidelines for identifying opportunities

In analysing the opportunities that database marketing opens up for a particular company, we focus first on two of the components of the profit equation, revenue development and defence; and cost reduction. These two components of company profitability provide an important link between the development of strategic marketing systems (including database marketing) and the company's business strategies and plans. Revenue development and defence and cost reduction are central themes of most corporate plans. Many of the opportunities opened up by database marketing affect both costs and revenue. Some lead to increased revenue while costs stay static or rise more slowly than revenue. Others lead to falling costs while revenue stays static or falls more slowly than costs. These effects will be achieved by the development and implementation of particular applications of database marketing, such as telemarketing, which are then used to change the way the company does business.

Many of the changes produced have a short and a long term dimension. For example, telemarketing may produce cost savings and revenue increases which arise relatively quickly through reducing the cost of contacting and selling to customers and by increasing market coverage. These shorter term effects are not of course once for all, but continue so long as the company continues the application. However, greater market coverage and reduced cost of coverage may allow a company to enter different product markets. The company may be able to sell a wider product range to existing customers. It may also be able to sell information resulting from the application.

We must therefore identify the types of revenue and cost changes that might result from different aspects of database marketing. We can analyse the effect on revenues and costs in many ways. The different approaches include the following:

1. By category of customer
2. By category of product
3. By application introduced (e.g. sales force support, inbound or outbound telemarketing, direct mail)
4. By category of change (i.e. whether it is cost saving, revenue defence or growth).
5. By time period (short, medium or long term).
6. By category of staff, function or marketing channel (e.g. impact on field sales force, sales offices, retail outlets, physical distribution, marketing communication, market research)

Note that the cost reduction and revenue increasing effects of some changes are not separable. If we get more revenue from a fixed cost base, we have reduced costs as a proportion of sales.

There is no single correct way to analyse cost and revenue effects. Much depends on the focus we wish to generate and on our judgement as to the strategic significance of the project. For example, if our main marketing problem is the rapidly rising cost and/or falling productivity of our field sales force, then channel productivity might be the best basis for analysis. If one of the main reasons for a company's inability to achieve its growth targets is lack of an effective and efficient channel for handling new categories of products, we might want to carry out the analysis in terms of the effectiveness of market coverage by different channels for different products.

In practice, a cross-tabulated classification may be needed to reflect different business priorities. This classification may be by cost or revenue effect by function, further tabulated by category of cost or revenue. The following are examples of possible effects, classified first by whether cost saving or revenue defending/increasing, and then by some marketing disciplines. This list is not meant to be comprehensive, but rather to suggest types of opportunity that should be considered.

Cost saving

Field sales force   Reduction in number needed for given market coverage, due to more efficient calling pattern and less time spent identifying prospects and obtaining prospect information; reduced staff support required, due to higher quality information available to sales staff; reduced systems support, due to unification of possible variety of support systems; reduced sales force turnover due to quality of support and consequent higher motivation; possibly broader span of management control and reduced number of reporting levels feasible, due to better standard of information on activites and effectiveness of field sales staff, leading to lower management costs.

Sales office   Reduced number of staff required to deal with given number of customers or support given number of field sales staff, due to reduction in time spent obtaining and collating information and more efficient prospecting systems; reduced costs of handling customer enquiries due to improved structuring of response handling mechanism, so that customer enquiries go to relevant destination more smoothly without passing through irrelevant hands, lower staff turnover due to higher level of support and consequent improved morale; broader span of control and reduced number of reporting levels feasible, due to better standard of information on activities and effectiveness of office sales staff, leading to lower management costs; reduction in number of branch offices due to ability to cover market better and more 'remotely'.

Market research   Lower expenditure on external research, due to higher quality and relevance of information available on customers and prospects.

Marketing and business planning   Reduced costs of information collection and management, due to availability of higher quality, more relevant and updated information on customers and prospects, leading to possible reduction in numbers of planning staff or in planning component of other jobs.

Retail   Improved site planning, due to ability to match customer profiles to area profiles more accurately, possibly leading to need for fewer outlets to attain given revenue targets; lower surplus inventory, due to ability to target 'sale' merchandise marketing; higher utilization of space, due to ability to market special in-store events to database.

Product marketing   Reduced costs of selling, due to better attunement of existing and new channels – some of which are only possible using database marketing – to customer needs.

Marketing communications   Lower costs for achieving any given task, due to greater accountability and to improved ability to identify targets for communication and make communication relevant and therefore more effective.

Inventory   Reduced write-offs due to reduced frequency of launch of inappropriate products and to earlier termination of dying products; general improved forecastability of marketing campaigns, leading to reduced temporary inventory peaks for given products.

Revenue defending or increasing

Field sales force and sales office   Higher revenue due to ability of sales staff to concentrate calling on higher revenue prospects; less lost business and fewer lost customers due to improved customer care, as database marketing provides improved channels for customers to signal needs; enhanced new product revenues due to improved ability to target customers for new products and eventually consequent greater ease of launching new products; greater ability of sales force to handle broader product portfolio, due to deployment of response handling system to inform relevant customers prior to the sales call.

Market research   Greater ability to identify potential for increased revenue among existing customers.

Business and marketing planning   More coherent plans to address new revenue opportunities, due to higher quality and relevance of information, leading to higher success rate with launch of new products, greater matching of distribution channels to customer needs, etc.

Retail   Ability to market additional products to existing retail customers, whether at retail or through mail order, due to quality of customer information; higher sales volumes of existing products due to ability to target promotions.

Marketing communications   Greater effectiveness of communicating with customers and prospects, leading to higher revenue for given cost.

Product marketing   Reduced costs of selling, due to better attunement of channels to customer needs, leading to ability to capture higher market share through lower prices.

Inventory   Lower stock-outs and therefore quicker inflow of revenue and reduced loss of sales to competition due to improved sales forecasting.

Guidelines for strategic appraisal

Once the opportunities have been identified, a strategic appraisal of their effect on the business is required. Not every database marketing application is appropriate for every company. The right mix of applications and the correct phasing of their implementation is determined by:

- Business factors, such as the company's objectives and current performance relative to them, the size of the company, the number of customers it has and the amount and frequency with which they buy, the type of products or services marketed, the types of channel through which they are marketed, the position of the different products in their life cycle, the company's market share and the state of competition.

- Technical factors, such as the company's commitment to investment in IT, the mix of applications already in place, the state of maturity of these applications, and the state of development of technology at the time the decision is being taken.

The need to justify (often on a relatively short term basis) is often seen as a barrier to implementing database marketing, particularly in companies which are not aware of the total costs of their current way of marketing. Sometimes, this is because the costs of marketing are spread across a number of different functions, such as finance (e.g. cost of customer credit and its collection), physical distribution (e.g. costs of storing finished goods and getting them to customers), business planning (e.g. market research) and customer service.

Fortunately, there is a well tried approach to the rather complex problem of quantification. The steps involved in quantification are shown in Figure 4.2 and are as follows:

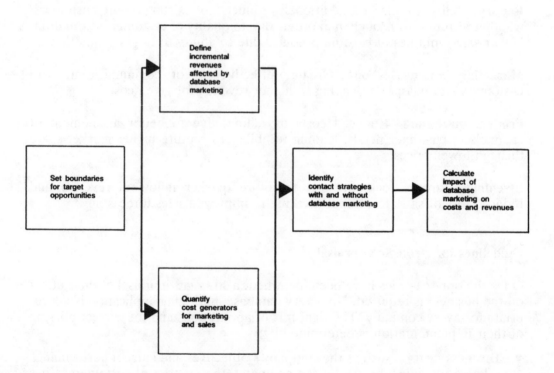

Figure 4.2: Steps in strategic appraisal

1. Target opportunities

A shortlist of target opportunities is generated, usually in management work-shops. This may be supplemented by a series of management interviews and discussions. Many of the best ideas are usually already present in the company, but have not been allowed to emerge because of the way in which policies are planned and implemented. After all, many database marketing applications are the implementation of commonsense ideas through the use of modern infor-mation technology. The outcome of this step is a statement of the target oppor-tunities. This provides the focus for the rest of the analysis.

2. Incremental revenue from database marketing

We must also take into account existing marketing plans. These should be reviewed to identify long term revenue growth objectives and to clarify the basis for revenue growth plans. Revenue growth plans may be based on factors such as overall market growth, specific marketing strategies (product range, price, distribution, advertising, etc.), or anticipated competitive changes. This analysis will indicate the areas where database marketing may generate revenue growth through improving the effectiveness of policies that are already planned.

3. Quantification of cost effects

Quantifying the cost savings from implementing database marketing before implementation is not easy. It is more difficult if the company's existing marketing information is not well organized. As many potential users of data-base marketing have only recently adhered to the marketing creed, the infor-mation required to quantify cost effects may have to be estimated. This may require not only 'reconstruction of figures', based on estimates of staff, but the use of pilot studies, where particular applications are implemented.

Typically, a comprehensive exercise to gather and analyse cost information is required. It will normally cover every channel of communicating with and distributing products and services to customers, such as sales force, sales offices operating by telephone and mail, retail outlets, media advertising, and direct mail. The aim is to quantify costs which may be changed by database marketing approaches. This exercise is based on interviews, questionnaires, and analysis of financial and operating information relating to the channels of communication and distribution. This analysis may have to be carried out by market sector and product line as well as for the whole business, as some of the opportunities may be confined to particular products or sectors.

For example, suppose that we want to estimate the cost reducing effects on a sales force. The data we need include:

- Sales force activity analysis, to find out how sales staff are spending their time, in particular time spent on low productivity activities, such as prospecting and converting low potential customers, compared with time spent on high productivity activities (time spent converting high potential customers or preventing their loss)

- Sales revenue productivity statistics, to measure the productivity of the time actually devoted to customers.
- Data on market size (overall and by product – number of customers and revenue potential), to enable us to estimate the proportion of the market (overall or for given products) left uncovered by the sales force.
- Data on how the activity profile of the salesforce changes when we implement database marketing and put relevant applications (e.g. telemarketing, direct mail) to work.
- Data on the current costs of managing the sales force.
- Information on how the activities which generate these costs affect the productivity of sales staff.
- Information on how database marketing disciplines will lead to a change in the nature and scale of these activities (e.g. data provision work by support staff).

With these and other data, we can then calculate the cost effects. Our estimates will obviously have a degree of uncertainty attached to them, so we may need to discount revenues by a risk factor.

4.   Contact strategies

For each main opportunity area and for each planned policy, the current method of contacting customers should be determined. Future contact strategy options, using database marketing, should then be identified, and an assessment made of:

- The capability of existing channels to support revenue growth targets and the cost of resourcing those channels to achieve them
- The incremental cost of the database marketing strategy needed to support the revenue growth target.

5.   Revenue and cost review

A summary of marketing activity over the period of the plan should then be prepared. This should show the effect on costs and revenues of employing existing methods to achieve targets, and compare it with the costs and revenues implied by the use of database marketing. This should show the areas where database marketing is more effective.

If our analysis indicates the need for distribution channel change underpinned by database marketing, the result might be a wholesale change in the revenue/cost profile. Whole categories of cost may disappear (e.g. the abolition of sales branches) and new ones appear (e.g. their replacement by a central sales coordination unit). Distribution channel change may create further strategic marketing opportunities, such as the ability to address whole new markets or launch completely different types of product. However, the change may be less revolutionary e.g. the refocusing of a calling sales force on larger customers and the replacement of their efforts by a telemarketing operation.

In this area, the questions that face us are:

- How large are the opportunities represented by a database marketing-driven change to distribution channels?
- Can our company's organization, culture and processes cope with the forces set up by the change? For example, if sales and marketing staff have not been completely revenue accountable, what will be the effect of giving a large part of the business to a profit-accountable channel?

The decision conference

Database marketing is not an all or nothing affair. The revenue and cost analysis must show what options are available, in particular the revenues and costs of implementing specific applications more or less widely. These options need to be evaluated against short and long term business priorities. Eventually, choices must be made. Because the new marketing approach is likely to cut across internal political boundaries, a mechanism for achieving consensus must be established.

Therefore, the final step in reaching a decision about implementing database marketing is to hold a workshop, bringing together senior decision makers in an intensive, interactive environment. Here, they focus on the strategic appraisal and its implications for marketing and for systems investment. The event can vary in format and time required. Typically, it lasts from half a day to two days. It is designed to work through all the issues in a systematic way. The workshop is an integral part of the strategic appraisal process. After the workshop, a summary document is prepared. This merges the results of the appraisal with the decisions taken at the workshop and makes recommendations for board level decisions.

Database marketing may afford many opportunities for increasing revenue and reducing costs, but unless these opportunities are firmly built into operating plans as targets, they are unlikely to be achieved. As many database marketing systems are implemented at the behest of marketing or sales functions, which do not control some of the areas in which revenue and cost opportunities may arise, there needs to be agreement with the appropriate revenue- or cost-responsible functions concerning how revenue and cost opportunities are to be captured. It is therefore important for these functions to be involved in the whole strategic appraisal process.

5 Strategy and systems

Successful implementation of database marketing depends on building a bridge between marketing and systems management. There are four areas where effort and attention should be focused if strategy is to be formulated and implemented successfully:

- The database marketing strategist must 'think big', in terms of a corporate systems architecture, of which database marketing is an integral part.
- The long term focus of business and systems analysis should be the revenue streams that arise from use of the customer database, not the potential sales of individual products, business processes, information flows or databases.
- Effort should be split 80:20 between data applications and database management, not the other way round.
- Pragmatism and realism must underpin this division of effort. Investment of effort should be based on what is likely to work and deliver results, not on what would be nice to have.

Marketing architecture

Working with a comprehensive corporate systems architecture helps marketing management work harmoniously with systems management and the rest of the business. The objective of the systems architect is to show the framework within which information in its broadest sense flows. The meaning of 'systems architecture' can be illustrated by starting with a simple picture of the ideal role of marketing – as the integrator between customer and company (see Figure 5.1).

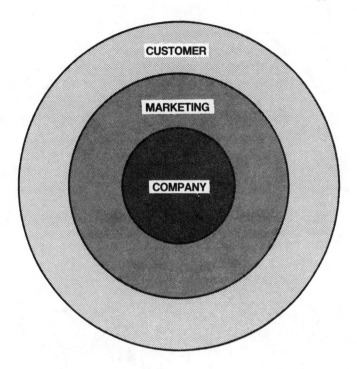

Figure 5.1: The marketing function as integrator between customer and company

This is a simple marketing textbook vision of the role of marketing. It is an admirable vision, but difficult to achieve in practice. It begs many questions about the way in which marketing should act as the integrator in practice, both on a day to day basis in relations with customers, and in the long term, when it comes to determining corporate strategy. The way to answer these questions is to develop a vision of the information flows which justify this picture.

If we superimpose some information flows on our simple picture, two main flows become apparent: customer flowing and inward flowing (see Figure 5.2). A coherent database marketing architecture requires development of the right applications for the system to work at the interface between company and customer. Some examples are shown as bubbles in the diagram. The framework determined by the specifying of these applications determines the marketing system architecture. Put simply, we must determine the applications before we determine the architecture, as these determine what information flows need to take place, in what form, and so forth. Otherwise, we run the risk of developing a system which looks good in theory, but does not meet the needs of the business in practice.

The architecture therefore defines how and when information flows at every

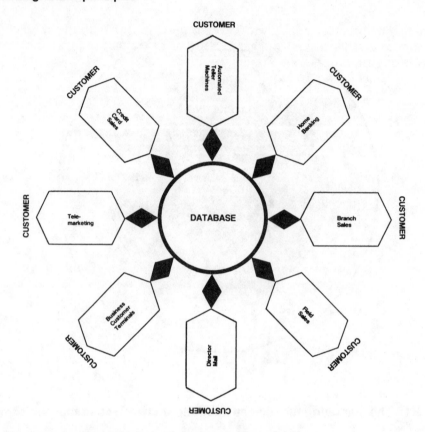

Figure 5.2: Marketing systems architecture in banking

stage of the marketing function's cycle of planning, executing, monitoring and reporting. This architecture represents the corporate view of the database marketing process. The need for this architecture cannot be over-emphasized. Database marketing systems are not small systems development items. They cannot be treated as a set of smaller sub-systems (e.g. a telemarketing system, a system for mail shots, a customer service system and a customer research system) which can be built up over time into a bigger coherent system, without the guidance of a corporate marketing architecture. If we approach the design this way, we may to face serious problems when we try to make these sub-systems work together.

Revenue streams

The right approach to creating the corporate marketing architecture runs counter to the normal inclinations of systems management. The approach to defining the architecture begins with *revenue analysis*, not with the more conventional *data analysis*. In our experience, the most difficult part of the revenue analysis is determining what a company's future revenue streams will look like, as opposed to its current revenue streams. These streams are determined by:

- The types of customer the company will be serving in the future
- The products they will be customers for
- How the company will serve them (i.e. through which kinds of marketing channel)
- How the revenue will flow through the channel

Figure 5.3 illustrates these concepts.

For example, the automated teller machine as used in banking may be seen from a systems management perspective as an inspired data analysis and management creation. It is a much more efficient way of generating data about transactions, but the marketing architect views it as the first step in the creation of a variety of future revenue sources. It is a new medium for marketing communications, or even a new marketing channel. Through it, new products can be marketed, and new ways to improve customer satisfaction can be implemented.

Examples of revenue streams abound in the world of classic direct marketing. Most campaigns aim to develop or cultivate revenue streams. Individual direct marketing applications, such as lead generation and qualification, telemarketing,

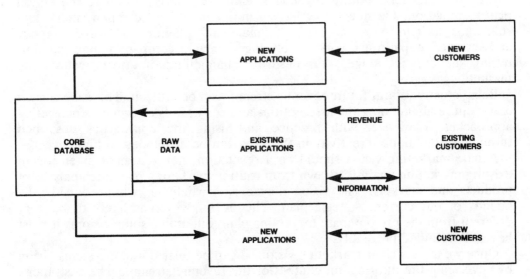

Figure 5.3: The marketing vision

multi-media contacts and catalogue marketing, all generate revenue streams. These streams can be developed further by running the applications off a corporate marketing database and by applying database marketing techniques.

We focus on revenue-driven rather than data-driven approaches because of:

- The need to cost-justify and prioritise development. There must be a clear revenue stream arising out of every application, against which the costs involved in developing the application can be set.
- The risk inherent in a technical data-driven approach, which might produce a system which not only yields very little incremental revenue and profit, but actually damages our marketing effort and reduces profits.

Because of the cost of developing applications, system development priorities should be set from a hard-nosed business perspective. Fortunately, revenue stream analysis lends itself to analysis in terms of return on investment. The costs and benefits of every application that is part of the corporate marketing architecture must be quantified.

Creating the vision

The most difficult part of the revenue stream approach is creating the vision. For many companies, this task is carried out by external specialists, such as an advertising or direct marketing agency. As the database marketing approach receives wider acceptance, it is becoming clear that the task cannot be left entirely to outsiders. Future revenue stream analysis is central to marketing plan formulation. Outsiders may have a major input, but company marketing staff must start to 'own' this aspect of marketing planning. However, agency and systems people must work closely together with company marketing staff during the creative stage, thus ensuring channelling of effort towards the feasible.

Being creative about future revenue streams can be difficult. This is because it may require abandoning the assumptions and constraints of previous marketing approaches. However, with practice and using the approaches described throughout this book, creativity in this area can be developed to high levels.

A true marketing vision should be a revelation, not a straight extension of existing marketing analysis, drawn from routine marketing planning analyses of products and markets. The vision may exist partially or wholly outside the bounds of our current stategic plan. The overall vision is likely to be very different from the pre-database marketing plan, but unlike some visions, it must be firmly founded on reality.

Once we have a clear marketing vision, it can be turned into a systems vision by envisaging the information content of the revenue streams. The customer's dialogue with us is multifunctional. He is in dialogue not just with sales and marketing staff, but also with operational staff. In a bank, these would include counter and back-office staff and head office staff.

Information arises from each contact. Sometimes, a step in the dialogue is invisible to us e.g. when the customer picks up a brochure or catalogue that he requested but laid aside until he had time to consider it. We need to think how information and then revenue can be made to flow from every step in the dialogue, not just from the normal direct marketing flow. We must think how it can be coaxed out of customer by giving them the appropriate incentives and benefits at every stage.

The alternative to the revenue driven approach is the data driven approach. This is fine for analysing past performance. However, it leads to the problem of 'data in search of an application'. This is wrong for database marketing, which aims to develop needed data as part of the process of revenue creation.

Suppose, for example, you are a bank marketing manager responsible for developing the market for home improvement loans. The systems department is likely to take a data-driven approach to your problem. They will look at the data available and see which elements will help you. They may suggest acquiring consumer demographic data and using these in conjunction with past purchasing behaviour for bank products. Their conception of your needs is constrained by their retrospective view of the data.

A revenue-driven approach looks for new ways to generate revenue streams and may hit upon home mover data derived from other sources, and ways in which the bank can work (perhaps with other parties) to generate these data. The next step will be to consider what revenue can be made to flow from the relationship between the bank and those who are about to or have just moved. This is likely to lead to a change from the simple product marketing approach (selling home improvement loans) to a customer-oriented approach (developing revenue and information flows out of a dialogue with a particular group of customers). The end result of this may be entry into different businesses, such as additional kinds of insurance, estate agency, and perhaps even to the provision of a comprehensive financial and property services package for these customers (subject to consistency with corporate strengths and weaknesses relative to competition, of course).

The 80:20 resource rule

The resources used in system development must be split 80:20 between applications and database. This follows from our revenue stream message. The vision of how the business will work is not just a database vision. In terms of system development effort, this is barely 20 per cent of the vision.

The real vision relates to marketing applications or, in simple terms, what we can do with our database to acquire, develop and defend customers. Senior marketing management must be involved in its development, working closely with their staffs and external agencies. This is because it lies at the core of commercial strategy. Senior marketing management must develop an understanding of marketing as a strategic and tactical system, based upon customer dialogue. In the initial phases of adoption of database marketing, external agencies may need to educate senior managers so that they can develop this vision. But it is not a tactical vision of promotions and short term extensions of product lives. It is definitely a strategic vision.

In developing this vision, systems management must help. They are needed to define a function systematically in systems terms (objectives, task, inputs, outputs, connections with other functions, etc.). They are used to employing these definitions to work out business opportunities. It is the role of marketing management to ensure that systems management set their priorities and spend their time according to the 80:20 rule.

Developing the applications part of the vision involves the following steps:

1. Business review (identifying future revenue streams)
2. Applications definition (how to achieve the revenue streams)
3. Database definition (data needed by the applications systems)
4. Analytical functions (reports, planning support, etc.)

Eighty per cent of the effort and budget must go on the first two tasks. The pay-off comes from applications, not the database itself. A sure sign of 'database focus' from the systems department is undue emphasis on data modelling. If you are shown a diagram like Figure 5.4, BEWARE. While data modelling can be of value, you need to be sure that systems staff do not spend all their creative energy producing data models to the detriment of application development.

Because of the costs of developing and testing applications, it is important to understand the applications that are most likely to enhance revenue and profit streams. These range from stand alone direct marketing activity, to integrated support of all channels to achieve and sustain a dialogue with customers. The applications are the main components in a system whose objective is large scale relationship management. These are the applications that systems management define in computing terms. They include:

● Market definition, segmentation and prioritization
● Targeting
● Enquiry management
● Managing post-enquiry dialogue
● Fulfilment
● Definition, analysis and choice of contact strategies

Like many systems, a true database marketing system depends on feedback. This is true at individual level (from customers during dialogue) and at the aggregate level (relating to the effectiveness of particular policies and applications). Database marketing is a true virtuous circle – the better you do it, the better you become. Therefore, a prerequisite of any system design is the

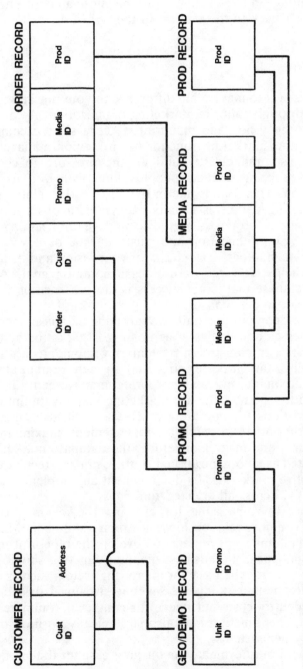

Figure 5.4: Beware data modelling

provision for incorporation of feedback. The marketing vision must include ensuring that customers provide the required information as part of the dialogue with them. Marketing and sales staff must be motivated to ensure that this information does get back to the system, in the right form.

Organizational change

If database marketing is to make a big difference to your marketing, you cannot continue to work through your old marketing organization. A coherent team is required to create the vision and blueprint. Otherwise, the commitment and motivation within the marketing function or in senior management will be lacking. You are also unlikely to build up the pressure to change systems practices. You must bring systems people along with you to develop and implement the vision. This sounds fine in theory, but the relationship between systems and marketing people is usually fraught with obstacles. Each side's opinion of the other is prone to prejudice and generalization. Each uses a different language. Communication and trust must be deployed to overcome barriers erected by technology. The clarity of your vision and its acceptance by top management helps. It gives both sides a common goal. An additional requirement for database marketing success is the presence of a strong senior manager acting as a project sponsor.

The company must commit to a unitary marketing database, feeding off other functional databases as automatically as possible. Marketing system development must be part of mainstream system development, not a backwater attracting low quality staff, little resource and no management attention.

The gap between marketing and corporate management, relating to the resources required for a true database marketing system, the interpretation of benefits and implications for operating practices, must also be overcome. To ensure maximum support from corporate management, maximum cooperation from other functions, and maximum return, the database marketing approach must be implemented as an organizational culture, not as a technique to develop slightly more effective marketing. Its development and implementation must be planned strategically, across all affected functions.

Marketing is clearly responsible for creating the vision – of customers, markets, revenue streams, relationships and their fulfilment. Marketing must work closely with systems management to develop the blueprint for the system itself. In larger companies, the business planning function should measure the size of change, and provide the basis for measuring factors such as the efficiency of customer contact. This may involve revenue stream analysis followed by a contact audit, to identify customer needs for contact if commercial objectives are to be attained. This function may also strategically position the marketing system relative to other systems.

Senior management must evaluate the business case for the marketing system, as the only authority which can legitimate it as the company's central marketing approach. They must allocate resources and funds, reflecting the 80:20 applications:database split. They must decide whether the time and internal resources available dictate the need to use external resources. Senior management must also decide who controls the marketing D.P. budget. The control should probably be shared between marketing and systems functions. In many cases, budgets may be switched from above the line activity. The size of the systems development budget may look frightening relative to marketing staff budgets, but not in relation to media budgets. The budget should be judged against the amount of turnover and profit managed through the system.

Senior management must take responsibility for achieving the cultural change required to make relationship marketing a way of life for the whole business. This demands communications programmes and retraining as well as changes to the business policy process. The personnel function should be involved.

The art of the possible

Having prepared the blueprint, the company must be realistic and develop a sense of perspective about what can be achieved with today's computer systems. It is important to be realistic about revenues and costs. Revenue forecasts must relate to past examples and case histories. Direct marketing agencies can normally provide these. For example, automation can reduce inventory cost, management time and costs, or advertising wastage.

Benefits and costs must be evaluated strategically, taking into account the company's position relative to competition. The aim is improvement relative to competition, not perfection. This applies particularly when it comes to determining the timeframe of the investment and the return. Each step in the process must be identified. In particular, the costs of each step must be evaluated against the willingness to commit the investment. The costs and benefits of a comprehensive database marketing system are great. Without top level support, implementation may be stopped by costs, politics or inertia.

Software packages usually indicate the state of the art in feasible information systems. If a company is trying to do something way ahead of them, it is not likely to succeed. Databases should be built to performance, not aesthetic criteria. Large volumes of data must be delivered – the hardest test of a database system. Systems specialists should not be allowed to decide on an aesthetic design unless they can prove it will deliver at high volume. This problem can easily be underestimated. There are unlikely to be any packaged solutions to meet all a company's application needs, so it will be necessary to integrate several independent solutions. The technical problems of integrating applications and the central database will be hard to overcome.

Designing and implementing the system

Systems professionals must evaluate the feasibility of implementing the concept developed by marketing management. They must also be closely involved in drawing up the blueprint. To understand the marketing concept behind the system, they may need some education before they are able to assess the system, and see where the concept needs to be changed to enhance feasibility without reducing its coherence.

Large strategic projects require tough management and clear methodologies. If a company does not have a clear marketing architecture from the beginning, it is likely to hit trouble. Suppliers must know that missed deadlines are not acceptable. Projects must be kept small, and if in doubt, split. They should be piloted or tested wherever possible. Disasters tend to occur with large unwieldy projects with no benefits until they are finished and most of the costs incurred at the beginning. It is important to deliver a series of marketing benefits throughout the project. This will make expenditure easier to justify and help guarantee the cooperation of company management. Large systems expertise is required before a company embarks on a comprehensive database marketing system. Users and beneficiaries of the system should be communicated with and trained, to ensure that they enjoy the benefits you are creating.

Managing the system

Fully computerized marketing is powerful. If this power is misdirected, dramatic mistakes can be made. Millions of letters can and have been mailed in error, with the wrong offer or to the wrong customer. In a company with branch sales offices, branch management and staff may be alienated. Marketing costs may escalate. The marketing organization and all its processes may need restructuring to deal with this new way of marketing and to ensure quality and accountability. Field and central marketing and sales resources will need to be more flexible, to capture opportunities signalled by the high speed system. Campaigns will need to be planned quickly.

Field marketing resources must respond promptly according to the different contact strategies indicated by the system. This may imply tighter functional control of field marketing and less reporting into local general (i.e. branch) management. However, within this tighter control, some responsibility for managing the relationship with the customer may be delegated. This depends on how central resources can be made available to help a branch, what economies of scale are involved in campaign implementation, and whether the branch has the right skills and systems to manage the full relationship with the customer.

The marketing plan must be conceived in terms of dialogues and revenue and cost streams. Tactical and strategic marketing accountability must be defined in terms of successful, high quality and profitable dialogue with customers. A wider variety of strategic and tactical marketing approaches and skills will be needed to deal with customers with different needs and of different potentials. The skills of strategic marketers should be broader. They will need to encompass personal selling, sales promotion, advertising, product launching, lead generation, as well as general management skills such as planning, scheduling, forecasting and project management. These skills will be needed to blend multimedia campaigns for many different customer groups, working in an integrated fashion with other functions. The training implications for both marketing and systems staff are therefore substantial.

To summarise the points arising out of the above analysis:

1. Think big. Take the perspective of a corporate architect.
2. Think revenue. Work with agencies and systems management to create the vision of future revenue streams.
3. Think applications. Your systems people should work so closely with you that they create applications as if they were full members of the marketing team.
4. Think creativity. Use experienced systems people to identify where you are now, bring expertise in house from agencies and consultancies, and obtain board support for your vision.

6 Developing the approach

The idea of computerizing marketing is beginning to excite the interest of marketing directors and managers in a wide variety of industries. In the last few years, leading edge marketing companies have started to instal new computer systems to increase the efficiency and performance of marketing and sales staff.

These systems vary tremendously in their size. Some are small, operating on a single microcomputer. Some are massive, stretching the capacity of large mainframe computers. The use to which these systems are put also varies widely. Some are true database marketing systems, some are systems for telephone selling or sales reporting, and some are for working on aggregated market data (in which individual customers are not identifiable) to carry out market and competitive modelling and forecasting. Their importance to the company using them also varies. Some are 'nice to have', perhaps for dotting the i's and crossing the t's of long term forecasts. Others are at the core of marketing or sales policy, perhaps driving the company's whole sales effort or providing new understanding of a brand's customers and their likely response to a new pack size, variant or promotional campaign.

In all but a few companies, marketing is being computerized in a piecemeal way. The most important applications are computerized first, but without thought about how marketing and sales will be using computers in the future. However, the idea is slowly taking root that computerizing marketing should be planned.

This does not mean waiting until 'things (e.g. computer technology, the marketing department's structure) settle down', because they never do! It means taking a realistic view as to which applications will benefit from computerization, which ones are priority, and where the different computerized applications need to be linked in some way. In this chapter, we examine why computerising marketing is exciting such interest and suggest how a company considering whether to do it, or what its next step should be, should proceed.

But before we do this, we need to establish a clear view of what marketing does, seen from a systems perspective. Without this, it is difficult to plan ahead. The main components of a marketing system, seen from a non-technical, managerial perspective, are:

- A database, containing information about customers and/or markets, their behaviour and their reaction to our behaviour – our policies. It may also contain information about how we (and our competition) have behaved in the past. This database can be of many different kinds. Thus, that of a database marketer usually contains many individual customer records. A retailer's database may be based on sites and lines of merchandise. A brand manager's database may contain purchasing and other market data, aggregated from samples by different kinds of market segment.
- A set of analytical tools. These may be used for examining the database, so as to understand model and forecast customer behaviour. Or they may be used for evaluating policy options (e.g. for choosing which marketing mix is right for a particular segment).
- A policy process and structure. This provides a management framework for taking marketing decisions and making sure that they are implemented. Most marketing systems bear some relation to the 'classic' model of marketing decision making, which starts with consideration of corporate objectives in the light of the marketing environment (with the usual strengths, weaknesses, opportunities and threats analysis), and concluding with action plans for implementing particular changes to the marketing mix. This part of the system provides, if you like, the logical framework for the rest of the system.
- A set of policy instruments (the marketing mix) for specifying options and for delivering them to the customer. For manufacturers of branded consumer goods, these include different approaches to branding and ensuring that the product gets to the customer. For retailers, they include location, merchandising and display tools. For some industrial goods suppliers, they may include product design, sales force policy, and telemarketing.
- A set of physical mechanisms, which carry out policies and generate revenues. These include direct mail, telemarketing, physical distribution, and the sales force.
- A way of channelling information about marketing performance back to the database. Information may include customer purchases, sales returns, retail sales, market research, and customer satisfaction surveys.
- A control mechanism for monitoring the data and correcting policy to ensure that outcomes are consistent with objectives and plans.

This system, like many, is circular. Work done to improve the quality of the database leads to new policies. If the system is working well, when we implement these policies, we usually get further improvements to our information as well as improved marketing results. To put it another way, if we know our customers well, understand them, create the right products and services for them, and remember how they have received these services, we are in a better position to service these customers next time. In short, the marketing system is a virtuous circle.

The term marketing architecture refers to how we set out the many actions, processes and sets of information which constitute this virtuous circle. We must set them out clearly, understand them and identify how they are or should be linked together to optimum effect. This enables us to ascertain how and where computers can be used to increase marketing effectiveness. If the architecture is not well understood, computerizing individual aspects of marketing and sales will create severe difficulties later, when further aspects are ready for computerizing. The net result of this will be that the whole marketing system will yield far less than its full potential.

At this point, a marketing director might feel that his marketing situation changes so radically every year that there is no hope of making any progress on this front. But marketing creates an illusion of change, taking place at an ever increasing pace. If we distance ourselves from the hurly burly of today's market place, we notice a high degree of constancy in many markets. Most leading brands have led for years. The companies which are custodians of these brands have sustained their dominance by using a well established marketing approach which follows the tried and tested rules of good marketing.

But following these rules is not easy – markets always change, sometimes quickly, sometimes slowly. Marketers always have to adapt. Some of the changes taking place now are stretching the capacities of marketers to their limits. This is one reason why many marketing directors are looking to database marketing to provide a fundamental discipline and a system for managing their rapidly changing marketing environment and activities over the short and long term.

The four phases of development of database marketing

In theory, the marketing function should be the integrator between customer and company. To achieve this, marketing must supply information to the rest of the company, as well as workable policies. It must be a sort of 'information business' inside the company. Integration between customer and company depends on integration between marketing and other functions. For example, if a telemarketing call results in an order, confirmation should be available on-line that the product is available and deliverable by a certain date, and that the customer is cleared for credit purposes. Thus, the marketing database will need to be integrated with financial and physical distribution databases. Integration is therefore not a nice theoretical concept, but a 'hard' question of ensuring that information is available in the right place and used properly.

The marketing function must provide better information about customer behaviour and needs and the market to every business function that needs it – not just to marketing. For example, design and development needs information about customer needs and competitive offerings, production needs information on expected sales levels, distribution needs information on stock requirements and customer locations, and finance needs information on likely payment levels. Marketing must also provide a channel for information to flow from the company to its customers.

The aim of database marketing is to create and sustain a two-way flow of communication between the company and its customers. Achieving this requires the development and maintenance of information about customers and about the company's relationship with them. As marketing takes more and more seriously its role as an information provider, it moves closer and closer to absorbing database marketing as one of its main disciplines.

In large companies the volume and complexity of information flows demands the use of automation. A small company with few customers can keep all its customer information on paper and still provide all the information required by any function. The individual entrepreneur may even hold all this information in his head. However, most companies need to automate their marketing information just as they automate their production and financial information.

The marketing function also provides policy processes to use information (or to encourage its use elsewhere in the company) in making decisions, and resources to implement these decisions. Automating marketing information increases the amount of information available. Absorbing database marketing disciplines makes it possible to target narrower market segments. The net result is to make marketing a much more complex process, just as manufacturing has been made more complex by the increasing variety of production technologies and materials. The obvious response to this is to attempt to automate marketing itself. This is the objective of database marketing.

In any business function, automation tends to go in phases. In manufacturing, the phases were simple automatic production machinery, automation of whole production lines, computer aided design, and then computer integrated manufacturing. In marketing, we see four phases. These phases are not jumps. Each covers a broad spectrum of approaches. They evolve into each other, but their philosophy is very different. They are:

Phase 1.   Mystery lists
Phase 2.   Buyer databases
Phase 3.   Coordinated customer communication
Phase 4.   Integrated marketing

Figure 6.1 shows the main characteristics of these phases.

Growth process	PHASE 1	PHASE 2	PHASE 3	PHASE 4
Technology benchmarks	100% batch processing on external bureau	80% external batch processing 20% on-line processing	70% batch processing 20% on-line processing 5% minicomputer processing 5% personal computing	60% batch processing 25% on-line processing 10% minicomputer processing 5% personal computing
Applications portfolio	Direct mail	Direct mail, telemarketing sales support on separate databases at end user locations	Migration to central database with applications at end user location. Personal computing to support management control	Interfaces are established with non-marketing systems
Systems planning and control	Lax	More lax	Marketing management plan and control data resources and applications, and coordinate communication with customer	Database marketing as a profit centre, or value added user chargeback
Marketing organization	Specialization for learning direct marketing methods	Multiple organisation units independently developing buyer databases	Database marketing centre as centre of excellence and leadership and custodian of data	Database marketing centre has responsibility for strategy as well as tactical marketing planning
User awareness	Reactive and tactical. Senior marketing management is superficially involved	More reactive. Islands of middle marketing management develop isolated applications	Driving force: user is directly involved with data entry and data use	Participatory: user and database marketing centre are jointly accountable for data quality and for effective application
	PHASE 1 Mystery lists	PHASE 2 Buyer databases	PHASE 3 Coordinated customer communication	PHASE 4 Integrated marketing

Figure 6.1: The four phases of development

Phase 1. Mystery lists

Marketing databases are basic sales databases. They are often organised by product. A customer may appear many times under different product categories. It may be hard to identify that he is the same customer. These databases tend to grow from accounting systems – usually accounts payable. They are hard to analyse for marketing purposes, for example to identify good prospects for a particular product, or which customers are most likely to be susceptible to certain kinds of communication.

This phase has certain features relating to the company's overall attitude to marketing. There is usually conflict with other functions. They may not accept marketing's ideals. They may see marketing as a sideline. They see no reason for changing database structure to meet marketing needs. They may not even trust marketing. Sales forecasting may even be carried out by manufacturing.

If database marketing does exist, it is stand-alone. Lists of potential customers are bought in and not integrated with the sales database(s). They may be used once, to identify potential customers for a particular product, and then discarded. Other elements of database marketing are bought in. Campaign design (which customers are to be approached, how they are to be approached, how their responses are to be handled) may be bought in from a direct marketing agency. Telemarketing may be bought in from a specialist telemarketing agency. Fulfilment services (handling of customer responses and managing them through to their conclusion, e.g. the delivery of further information, the mail order delivery, the sales appointment) may also be subcontracted. Little is learnt from the providers of these bought in services – they are largely treated as 'black boxes' which help to make the sale.

In many respects, database marketing is at this stage tactical. It is not an integral part of marketing strategy. There may be no mention of database marketing when marketing strategies for a product or target market are under consideration. Direct marketing is more likely to be brought into play when line sales or marketing management is considering how to make its sales targets. Whether a campaign is successful or not does not affect the rest of marketing. Direct marketing is often driven by a particular sponsor. If he goes, database marketing may fall into disuse.

Phase 2. Buyer databases

In phase 2 sales and marketing databases are well organized, but there may be many databases. If a company uses several channels of distribution (a sales force, dealers, retailers), there may be different marketing databases for each channel. A specialist sales force might have its own database, because it goes more deeply into the particular factors that are important in its sector. Customer focus is possible – we can identify the nature of our relationship with a particular customer across different products. Databases can be analysed to develop strategy. For example, market penetration by product and sector can be analysed. Limited 'what-if' questions can be asked. There may be more than one marketing database. If so, each one may be incompatible with the others and with other sales and marketing systems.

Each database marketing campaign is well planned and executed in itself, but may overlap with other campaigns (e.g. different, even conflicting, products to the same market). This may be because each 'owner' of a marketing database regards the customers on it as 'his', even if the same customer appears on different databases. In very large companies, different originators of campaigns may simply not know what their colleagues are planning. So, for example, a bank customer may in this phase receive two communications on the same day, one seeking funds for a new investment for customers with idle funds, and one a loan product for those in need of instant cash.

Many leading marketing companies are in phase 2. In this phase, there is a strong focus on:

- *Broadening the database and improving its quality*. This may be by deepening the database (adding new kinds of information to it), or by encouraging stronger feedback from the sales force or from marketing campaigns, or by making sure that the feedback is entered quickly on to the database – an out of date database is a serious handicap in database marketing.
- *Target market definition*. As we saw earlier, the targeting of a marketing campaign is the most important element in database marketing. The best test of whether a campaign's target is the correct one is the response achieved by that campaign. With an improved database, it becomes easier to establish which markets are right for which products.
- *Improving list quality*. The list defines the customers in the target market who will receive the communications which are part of the campaign. There is never a perfect match between target market and list. We define our target market by criteria which we have established via testing to be the ones that determine which customers are the best prospects for our product, and then try to select a list of potential customers whose characteristics best match those of the target market. As our database improves in quality, this matching is higher quality. In addition, we can improve list quality by making sure that our data are of high standard, by removing duplicate entries and errors.
- *Segmentation and selection*. As our database improves and our experience grows, we become more creative about how we analyse our market data and how we use testing to improve our campaign success rate. Typically, much database marketing starts with fairly simple segmentation criteria. In industrial markets, establishment size and industry type are commonly used, together with product purchasing patterns. In consumer markets, product purchasing patterns are also used, together with socio-demographic characteristics. As our database improves, we may segment in industrial markets

by overall history of responses to campaigns, including purchases and other contacts, or type of decision maker, and in consumer markets by shopping habits.

- *Advanced scoring methods*. Marketing success depends not just on whether a company covers a market, but on how well it deals with customers who are the best prospects for a particular product. Companies therefore start to invest in scoring mechanisms, which are used to predict the likely behaviour of customers. The ability to do this depends not only on having a high quality database on customer behaviour, but also on developing statistical routines to provide the predictive tools and on the use of testing in every campaign. Note that we are not just trying to predict likelihood to buy, but also the likely response to individual elements of our marketing strategy. Is a particular customer more likely to respond to a cold sales visit than to a telephone call followed by a sales visit?

- *Offer design*. The offer – how the product or service is packaged to present its benefits to customers and cause them to respond – can now be developed. At this stage the company starts for the first time to look at its offerings from the customer's point of view. Direct marketing agencies make much of their contribution here, and in the following area.

- *Media choice*. As database marketing improves, the ability of a company to be specific about its target markets improves. It therefore needs greater expertise in choosing the media to reach its target markets. It also needs to understand how to combine media to greatest effect to manage potential customers through to the sale.

- *Response handling and fulfilment*. If a company improves its outbound marketing policies (communications to its customers), it also needs to improve its ability to handle the responses and fulfil them. Here, companies work hard to ensure that their handling of customer responses improves in quality and speed.

- *Testing*. Without testing, all the above improvements would almost certainly be ill-founded and temporary. Testing is the fastest route to improving the application of marketing disciplines in practice. Absence of testing is the fastest route to throwing away resources and losing credibility with top management. Testing is the only way we can know whether the criteria we are using to define campaigns and offers are the right ones.

- *Management systems to aid campaign planning and implementation*. With the volumes of data produced by marketing and sales databases, and the increased complexity of target markets, management needs to have some way of implementing its marketing campaigns more methodically. The first simple project management systems now appear, but typically on a product by product or market by market basis.

Database marketing is now a true part of the marketing mix, with a role in supporting other elements of the mix, for example:

- Enquiry handling for the sales force and customer service
- Providing the sharp edge to broad media advertising
- Providing a mail order channel.

Typical achievements may now include:

- More precise segmentation
- Sharper targeting
- Knowledge of the lifetime value of customers to the company
- Understanding of the effectiveness of combinations of campaigns
- Better closing of the sales loop
- Scoring methods to prioritize enquiries
- Team building within the marketing function.

Increased effectiveness without overall coordination leads to more conflict. The conflict may be within the marketing function, where campaigns for different products may clash. Different definitions of the same customer may be used for different databases (e.g. what is a major account?). The conflict may be with the sales function. The sales force may be deluged with leads it cannot handle. The salesman may carry his own database in his head, use it to drive his own campaigns, but will not divulge it or use anyone else's. The conflict may be with other functions. e.g. a campaign may cause inventory to run out. These conflicts are reduced by one database feeding off another (imperfectly or inter-mittently), one database incorporating another (then not serving all the needs of the original users of each database), or by managed, paper-based communication.

But phase 2 is a necessary phase. Most leading database marketing companies are here. All the systems building blocks for phase 3 are contained in phase 2:

- Mainframe databases and terminal-based marketing and sales systems
- Communications technologies
- Analytical input into planning

We learn from phase 2:

- Which data are important
- Which kinds of data we need to use together
- Which conflicts and stresses we must resolve
- How to use database marketing professionally

Phase 3. Coordinated customer communication

In phase 3, one database drives all customer communication and management. Computer systems are used to coordinate and drive campaigns. The emphasis is not on the database, though it is the powerful tool which makes it all possible. The emphasis is on customers – we start with the customer and work inward. Our first questions are:

- Who are our customers?
- What are their needs?
- How shall we plan and coordinate all our marketing efforts to meet these needs?

We work to answer these questions by:

- Using our own database
- Acquiring information from other sources
- Testing through pilot campaigns to establish customer needs
- Placing our results on our unitary database for access for different marketing purposes, but primarily for designing and implementing the campaigns which form our dialogue with our customers.

This powerful database creates problems. If we make it available to all marketers in a large company, the result will probably be too many marketing campaigns, usually overlapping and of diminishing effectiveness. In a multi-product, multi-channel company, this may be a serious problem. We therefore need a campaign coordination system. It may cover product managers, sales, advertising, telemarketing, product supply, store management and everyone involved in customer communication work. It ensures that all communication needs are identified, all campaigns notified to all relevant parties, all potential conflicts removed, and all resources available.

But in a large company, a campaign coordination system is not enough. We need other systems and programmes. For example, we need a campaign management system. This is because so many parties are involved in marketing campaigns that keeping them informed of campaign status before launch and ensuring that they all meet their deadlines is a huge task in its own right. The campaign management system ensures that all involved in a campaign know the schedule and complete their work on time.

We may also need a campaign planning system, which applies automated tools to identify and prioritize marketing opportunities. This system may be an expert system, feeding off the main database. We may need an internal communication programme, to ensure that staff, used to their old ways of marketing, understand the nature and rationale of the systems, and their role in making them work. We need a training programme, to ensure that staff can use the new systems.

How does phase 3 database marketing work? We start by planning the campaign, by using the database to identify a market gap and then to identify prospects within the target market, whose product and communication needs and behaviour we then research. We review relevant past performance, using the database's campaign analysis facilities. We further segment our target market, to determine how we are going to approach it. We identify possible contact strategies to meet customers needs.

Having finished this stage of analysis, we decide to launch the programme.

We enter the programme into the campaign coordination system. We are now working on detailed campaign design. We start to test. We devise pilot campaigns and run them to define, for example, the correct criteria for customer selection and choice of contact strategy. Our tests show us the best route to take. We finalize schedules and prepare for full implementation. The campaigns enter the campaign management system.

We inform other functions, particularly inventory, and get on with the task. The feedback, planned in to the campaign, continues until the end of the campaign. Then we use automated facilities to evaluate the campaign. All campaign information and evaluation automatically enrich the database.

Phase 4.   Integrated marketing

Many functions automate within closed loops, but they need each other's information for every part of their Plan – Execute – Monitor – Report cycle. Thus, inventory planners must receive reports on database marketing performance. It will never be possible to link every function automatically, so each functional 'subsystem' automatically gets the information it needs from every other subsystem. But we can go a long way to ensuring that links are made at relevant points in the cycle. Some links will be automatic (using the common architecture that we should establish right at the beginning). Some will be paper- (or even meeting-) based. Above all the system must be transparent, so that all involved know what should be done.

Our marketing strategy now combines the lifetime management of customers with the management of campaigns for particular products and services.

Where database marketing stands today

Database marketing has its roots in the world of direct marketing, where the needs of 'mass communication', broadly defined, led to the use of computerized marketing systems. However, this mass marketing is not to be confused with mass prospecting for new customers. Most direct mail and telemarketing activity takes place between companies and their regular customers.

The relative preponderance of 'customer dialogue' application may be because the use of unstructured and unqualified lists for prospecting is unproductive. As database marketing professionalism improves, we may see a rapid increase in the use of database marketing for prospecting. But there is a limit. Success in prospecting depends not just on the effectiveness of prospecting tools, but also on successful defence of existing customers by 'incumbents', who can also be presumed to be increasing their professionalism. Only in totally new markets (defined as areas of need where customers are currently not satisfied by any offer) will prospecting productivity be improved.

Today, few businesses understand the implications of recent developments in database marketing. There are two 'levels' of understanding:

1. Understanding the application of database marketing to marketing communication aspects of managing customer relationships.
2. Understanding the total database marketing approach, covering the complete marketing process, from planning through to implementation, in relation to every element of the marketing mix, not just marketing communication.

Marketing communications

Some businesses understand the importance of structured two-way communication with their existing and prospective customers as a way of managing their markets. The more advanced of these businesses are keen users of direct marketing and related techniques (e.g. the telephone as a tool for managing order taking and customer care), and these techniques are well integrated into the rest of their marketing mix. But some businesses are not so advanced. Even if they use modern techniques, the techniques are not well integrated with the rest of their activities, and may even conflict with them.

Full database marketing

The application of database marketing to managing the day to day relationship with individual customers and to planning communications campaigns is relatively well understood. The meaning of 'full database marketing' is only now beginning to emerge. Put simply, full database marketing involves running all marketing planning and action through the database and its associated analytical and planning tools. No full manufacturing, distribution or service business that we know actually does this, excluding some mail-order-only businesses. Eventually, however, a wide variety of businesses will be working in this way. These will include financial service businesses, certain retailers and many industrial equipment and supplies companies. This is the transition from day to day customer relationship management to customer relationship marketing.

7 Applications

The uses to which a database marketing system is to be put form the central part of the marketing vision. The creation of cost-effective, competitive and strategically significant applications is one of the biggest challenges faced by any company implementing a database marketing approach. The question such a company should ask is 'How can we use computerized customer data to support a significant and profitable dialogue with customers – now and in the future?'

The dialogue

The concept of dialogue is central to maximizing profit from customer data. A dialogue is more effective than a monologue. The customer is asked questions such as 'When do you intend to buy?', 'When will you next need help?' and 'What other products might interest you?' The responses are analysed by the computer and used to trigger future contacts. In this way, the database marketer can develop a dialogue with each customer, moving him towards purchase and ensuring that he remains satisfied after the purchase and that he purchases additional or replacement products later on. Without this, the result is a one way flow of promotional literature, most of which is wasted.

The computer is essential in ensuring that the right communication reaches the right customer at the right time. It selects the initial contacts. It analyses the customer response pattern. It plans the follow up. The aim is to have contact strategies to suit all customers and prospects, and to have computer applications that manage the execution of the contact strategy.

Types of application

The applications of database marketing can be described functionally, in terms of the type of marketing tools used. They can also be described in terms of policies (i.e. in terms of the marketing policy which the application supports). The functional description helps us understand the processes involved. The policy description shows how the various processes can be put together to achieve a commercial objective.

In this chapter, we have selected three applications by way of example. They are listed below, starting with a relatively simple application and moving to a more complex one. Between them, they illustrate all the key concepts and introduce some important technologies.

- A loyalty programme to customers served by a dealer network
- A programme to contact new customers
- An integrated approach to handling all new and existing customers

Loyalty programme

This example relates to a motor vehicle manufacturer who provides sales, service and spare parts through dealers. The dealers give customers a choice of competitive vehicles, so it is important for the vehicle supplier to measure customer satisfaction and competitive position. This information is used to bridge the gap between customer and supplier and to improve customer loyalty.

The contact strategy is based on a regular survey of customer satisfaction with the service provided by dealers' sales, service and parts departments. It involves the mailing of questionnaires to all private vehicle customers, two months after vehicle purchase, and two years after. Simplified examples of the questionnaires are given in Figures 7.1 & 7.2.

When the questionnaires are returned, they are dealt with as follows:

- The responses are evaluated so as to provide a customer satisfaction score, based on answers ranging from 'completely satisified' to 'very dissatisfied'.
- Requests from the customer to the dealer to make contact are passed to the dealer.

Dealers then contact customers who have low scores, or who request contact, and the result of the contact is recorded. Dealers find this information useful, and are enthusiastic users of the system. Each quarter, an analysis of the results is passed back to dealers for discussion. This helps to identify weak or disloyal dealers, so corrective action can be taken. The main technical requirements to operate this system are:

- A central database to store the customer data
- Computer terminals to enter them
- Follow up reports for dealers

1. ABOUT THE DEALER WHERE YOU BOUGHT THE CAR

	Location	Price	Recom mendation
Please put the following factors in order of their importance to you in your decision to buy your vehicle from this dealership (Put 1, 2 or 3 by the appropriate factors)	☐	☐	☐

2. ABOUT THE SALES DEPARTMENT

			Yes	No
Since taking delivery, have you been contacted by anyone from the sales department?			☐	☐

	Completely satisfied	Very satisfied	Somewhat dissatisfied	Very dissatisfied
How satisfied were you with your purchase and delivery experience?	☐	☐	☐	☐

3. ABOUT THE SERVICE DEPARTMENT

	Completely satisfied	Very satisfied	Somewhat dissatisfied	Very dissatisfied
How satisfied were you with the attention you received from the service department?	☐	☐	☐	☐

4. ABOUT THE PARTS DEPARTMENT

	Completely satisfied	Very satisfied	Somewhat dissatisfied	Very dissatisfied
How satisfied were you with the attention you received from the parts department?	☐	☐	☐	☐

5. ABOUT YOUR NEW CAR

Although you've only had your vehicle for a short time, please tell us how satisfied you are with the following points:

	Exterior (paint, trim)	Interior	Fuel economy	Overall
Completely satisfied	☐	☐	☐	☐
Very satisfied	☐	☐	☐	☐
Somewhat dissatisfied	☐	☐	☐	☐
Very dissatisfied	☐	☐	☐	☐

6. ANY ADDITIONAL COMMENTS

Figure 7.1: Customer loyalty survey after two months

1. ABOUT YOUR FUTURE PURCHASE PLANS

	Definitely	Probably	Probably not	Definitely not
When you next buy a new car, how likely is it that your will buy brand X?	☐	☐	☐	☐

	Definitely	Probably	Probably not	Definitely not
If you buy another brand, how likely is it that you will buy it from the dealer who sold you your current car?	☐	☐	☐	☐

2. ABOUT THE SALES DEPARTMENT

	Yes	No
Since taking delivery, have you been contacted by anyone from the sales department?	☐	☐

	Completely satisfied	Very satisfied	Somewhat dissatisfied	Very dissatisfied
How satisfied were you with the sales department?	☐	☐	☐	☐

3. ABOUT THE SERVICE DEPARTMENT

	Completely Satisfied	Very satisfied	Somewhat dissatisfied	Very dissatisfied
How satisfied were you with the attention you received from the service department?	☐	☐	☐	☐

4. ABOUT THE PARTS DEPARTMENT

	Completely satisfied	Very satisfied	Somewhat dissatisfied	Very dissatisfied
How satisfied were you with the service given by the parts department?	☐	☐	☐	☐

5. ABOUT YOUR NEW CAR

Now that you've had your vehicle for about two years, please tell us how satisfied you are with the following points:

	Exterior (paint, trim)	Interior	Fuel economy	Overall
Completely satisfied	☐	☐	☐	☐
Very satisfied	☐	☐	☐	☐
Somewhat dissatisfied	☐	☐	☐	☐
Very dissatisfied	☐	☐	☐	☐

6. ANY ADDITIONAL COMMENTS

Figure 7.2: Customer loyalty survey after two years

- Analysis reports for dealers
- Printers to produce the reports

In its simplest form, the system provides no on-line access to dealers. Information is provided in the form of paper reports. In our next example, on-line data is a key component of the system.

Contacting customers

This application uses a combination of telemarketing and mail to contact new customers. The contact strategy aims to achieve a structured dialogue with customers, with the following objectives:

- Gathering information on customers' widely varying needs and wants
- Providing information to customers to demonstrate how their needs and wants can be met by the products and services offered by the supplier
- Selling directly to customers, and converting routine contacts into up-selling or cross-selling opportunities
- Building respect and relationship with customers through appropriate contacts, with the result that they naturally turn to the seller to meet their needs.

Gathering information is as important as making sales for most telemarketing operations. Customers are not usually ready to buy on first contact. If information is gathered about their future needs, a cold contact can progressively be warmed up and moved towards a sale. Telemarketing contact can offer list validation and enhancement, to validate existing data and add new data such as some of the more elusive psychographic data. The latter relates to how customers think and feel – often approximated to behavioural data, which shows the outcome of how people think and feel in their behaviour.

Providing information to customers is also important. This can be done using both literature and telephone dialogue to handle customer enquiries. A contact strategy with the following structure may be appropriate:

- Direct response campaign to generate enquiries, with both coupon and telephone response
- Coupon data entry, and mail follow-up, or
- Telephone enquiry handling and qualification, and mail (literature) follow up
- All enquiries are scored and assigned a follow-up priority
- Follow-up by telephone or mail according to priority.

The use of the telephone can convert routine customer contacts into sales opportunities. Such opportunities occur when customers make routine calls for service, or when they call to ask for details of new products and services.

The technical requirements to operate such a system are more complex than in the loyalty programme. They are:

- Central database to store the customer data
- Data import facilities from external lists, to create the prospect file
- Computer terminals (VDUs) to enter coupon data
- Telemarketing subsystem
- More sophisticated scoring and reporting capabilities.

The telemarketing subsystem can be built using packaged software, which is now available from many sources. There are three main families of this kind of software now on the market:

- Outbound list processing software
- Inbound call management
- Account management

The outbound list processing software has been developed primarily for consumer marketing. It is designed for the semi-skilled telemarketer, of the type usually found in telemarketing bureaux. Typically, it runs on minicomputers. Features which are common include outbound list management and automatic dialling.

Inbound call management software has also been developed primarily for consumer marketing. It is oriented towards companies just embarking on tele-marketing and concerned to exploit an already existing volume of incoming calls. Typically it runs on minicomputers. Features which are common include script processing and inbound call management and distribution.

The account management software is oriented towards business-to-business use. It is aimed at the sales professional, not the semi-skilled telemarketer. Features which are common include outbound list processing, account manage-ment, and simple integration of telephone and computer. Common features of all these kinds of software are:

- Interface to core database
- Data collection and validation
- Simple order taking
- Performance reporting.

While it is possible to manage a telemarketing operation using software such as that described above loosely linked to a core database, there is a trend towards closer integration of the systems, such as:

- Core database on-line to the telemarketer
- Usage of the same software beyond the telemarketer (e.g. by the field sales force)
- Connectivity to related applications (e.g. window to order processing or other transaction systems).

Figure 7.3 summarizes how a telemarketing operation works. Figure 7.4 gives an overview of a typical telemarketing configuration.

The fully integrated system

An example of a fully integrated system is shown in Figure 7.5. At the centre is the customer database. If the organization is multi-branch or multinational, then this database may have central and local elements. Where these are and how they are used depends on the degree of variation between local and central campaigns, the costs of communicating data and of distributing computing equipment to handle local databases.

The components of the different applications are shown around the database. Specialist support staff work with company management to plan and help implement campaigns. Leads generated by the system are farmed out to the appropriate channels.

Lists of various kinds are used to help build the database, and are generated from it as the basis for tests and full campaigns. Leads and enquiries from various sources (e.g. mail, telephone, branch customer service) are handled using pre-tested contact strategies, and the results placed on the database, which leads to firm orders being placed with the distribution function. Marketing analysis is carried out to show the profitability of different approaches and to allow tactical changes to be made to campaigns currently being undertaken.

Stepping through the system

One of the main justifications for database marketing is that it serves the needs of marketing managers who have responsibility for particular groups of customers (or the entire market) or for particular products. These are the 'internal customers' of database marketing. One way to understand how a fully fledged database marketing system works to serve the needs of 'internal marketing customers' is to go through the steps by which a campaign is designed and implemented. The following description does just that. The channel of distribution being used is a direct sales force.

1. A marketing plan for a brand, product or sector is formulated. It identifies the need for one or more marketing campaigns. Preliminary work is carried out to to identify which kinds of campaign are likely to be most successful for the product or sector, and which customers should be targeted in them.
2. A campaign brief is drawn up, including campaign objectives, targeting, timing, the precise nature of the product or service to be promoted, the offer to be made to the customers, the benefits, how the campaign will help build company brand values, the resources required to implement the campaign, the way in which the campaign's success will be measured and the expected returns. This brief is the basis on which all work is carried out and ultimately executed.
3. The brief is used to derive a campaign specification, which is entered

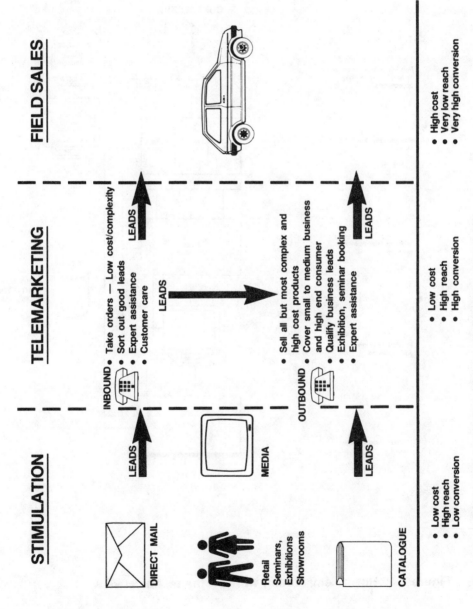

Figure 7.3: How telemarketing works – the functional view

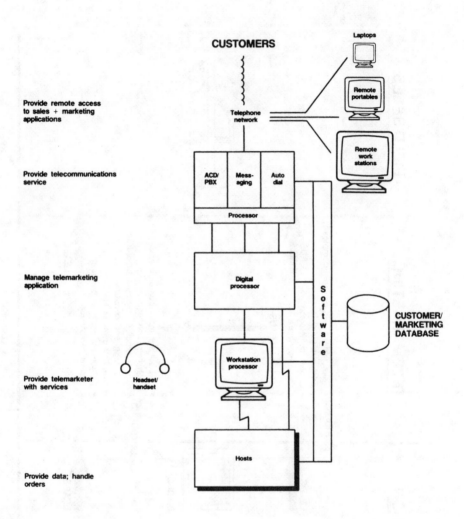

Figure 7.4: How telemarketing works – the technical view

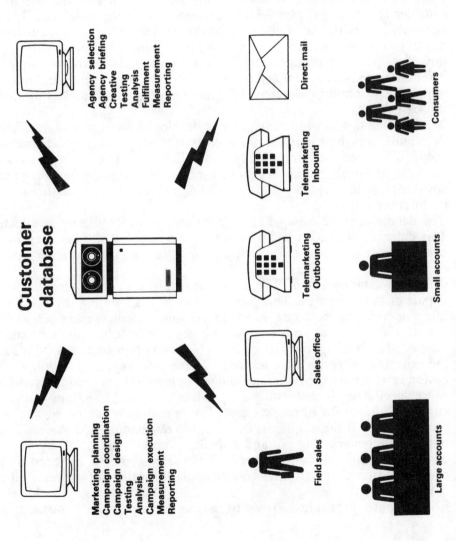

Customer database

Marketing planning
Campaign coordination
Campaign design
Testing
Analysis
Campaign execution
Measurement
Reporting

Agency selection
Agency briefing
Creative
Testing
Analysis
Fulfilment
Measurement
Reporting

Direct mail

Telemarketing Inbound

Telemarketing Outbound

Sales office

Field sales

Consumers

Small accounts

Large accounts

Figure 7.5: The fully integrated approach

into a computerized campaign coordination system. This coordinates the planning, execution and implementation of all marketing campaigns. It ensures that the approach to customers is coordinated and prioritized, taking into account the importance of different target markets, budget availability and the need to avoid clashes. One of its principal outputs is an agreed schedule of campaigns to be run. Without this, databased account management is impossible.

4. A campaign is designed to achieve the marketing objectives within the permitted budgets. Data about customers and past campaigns are used to define the target market more closely and to identify which broad kinds of campaign are likely to be most successful for the product or sector.

5. Campaigns are devised to test the different elements of the design on statistically significant sample lists extracted from the database. Testing normally covers the main elements of the campaign, i.e. which customers are targeted, which offers they receive, the timing of contacts with them, how they are to be reached and how their responses are to be handled.

6. The test campaigns are implemented and the results are analysed to determine which campaign elements (e.g. media, contact strategies) produced the best results.

7. The detailed design of the campaign is developed. As the contact strategy determines a high proportion of the costs of a campaign, contact strategies should be tested very thoroughly and prioritized. The tests provide the basis for prioritizing. This occurs in various ways, e.g. by including some customers in the campaign and excluding others, by handling customers in different ways.

8. The details of the campaign are agreed and an outbound list is selected. This determines which customers will be contacted in the first step in the contact strategy. The list is selected using a formula derived from analysis of tests.

9. The main campaign runs. The customer receives a communication which is part of the campaign. This prompts him to respond e.g. by coupon or telephone. If the response is to an inbound telemarketing set-up, the operator at the latter finds out which campaign or 'offer' the customer is interested in. The operator, cued by a sequence of on-screen displays, asks the customer a series of questions. These include confirmation of the customer's identity (possibly including telephone number, address and job title), specific needs concerning the product or service in question, and the customer's needs for further contact. The operator enters the answers into the computer. If the enquiry is by mail, the respondent is contacted by an outbound telemarketing call and a similar process takes place.

10. The enquiry information gathered from the customer is matched to the existing customer file (if any) and merged with other information on the database.

11. The computer uses rules derived from tests and agreed with the campaign

originator and project manager, to prioritize the enquiry according to the likelihood of a customer ordering. These rules are based partly on pre-determined campaign profiles (i.e. the kind of customer the company is trying to attract) and may use the data gathered during the customer's response.

12. A particular contact strategy is recommended, based on the type of product and on the priority.

13. The fulfilment organization receives information indicating, among other things, what kind of letter and additional material should be sent to the customer or, if the product is mail order, what product should be sent.

14. Local sales offices, sales staff or dealer outlets receive information about the enquiry on their computers, follow up enquiries, and feed the results of the follow-up back to the database.

15. The results of all enquiries and responses are analysed to provide regular reports on the effectiveness of activities and to help improve the effectiveness of future campaigns. Detailed performance data plus expenditure data from financial systems are used to evaluate financial performance and plan new campaigns.

This last example is database marketing at its best. It is an ideal which no fully integrated production and marketing company that we know of has yet attained, although several are planning to. Many companies realize that all the techniques and understanding to achieve this are available. The main barriers to it are internal. They include management understanding, motivation and commitment, defensive attitudes on the part of those managing existing channels of distribution and communications media, and the high set-up costs.

8 Contact strategies

Database marketing is one of the most precise marketing disciplines. It breaks the idea of developing a relationship with customers into a number of different tasks, and then builds the relationship by using a series of techniques which lead the customer to perceive that a smooth relationship is being developed.

Campaigns, contact strategies and treatments

The central task in relationship management via database marketing is the design and implementation of campaigns. Each campaign consists of a set of 'treatments' and associated 'contact strategies'.

A *campaign* is a planned set of marketing actions, aimed at meeting a particular set of needs of a defined group of customers. Thus, a campaign may aim to meet the mortgage requirements of single people with incomes over £50,000. Campaigns may be mounted within campaigns. For example, within the above campaign, a campaign might be mounted to meet the needs of these single people but only in certain geographical areas.

A *contact strategy* is a predefined set of actions to be used in handling customers. It starts with the initial contact and goes through to the conclusion of the particular phase in the dialogue, when the customer has either agreed to meet our objective (e.g. a purchase) or decided not to. Many contact strategies may be used in any one campaign. Figure 8.1 indicates the central role of the database in selecting the contact strategy.

A *treatment* is a step in a contact strategy. It often relates to the medium used for the first step in the contact strategy. In our example, treatments used may be an advertisement in the general press, or a mail shot or telephone call

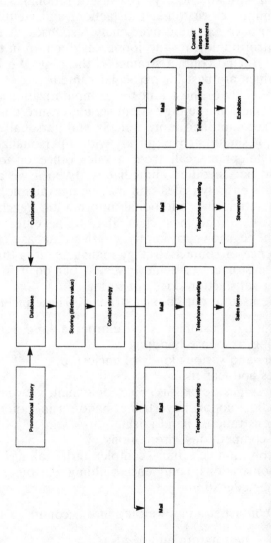

Figure 8.1: The role of the database in a contact strategy

to company directors. The optimum treatment is typically determined by the ability of particular media to reach target customers effectively. Later contact strategy steps are likely to be determined by the degree of customer interest and the complexity of the dialogue.

The contact strategy is an important element of database marketing. A good contact strategy ensures that our relationship with our customers is both high quality and effective. As we learn more about our customers, we learn which strategies are most effective in meeting their needs. Why do we formalize strategies? Why don't we leave it to customers to contact us, or to sales staff to decide how to deal with an enquiry? Because a rational, structured way of handling customers improves customer satisfaction, and yields the economies of a well planned approach executed over many responses. A planned contact strategy helps us control fulfilment – no loopholes open up in the way that we deal with customers. But no contact strategy is the best. We learn by testing and experimenting which are best for particular campaigns.

One of the main benefits of most kinds of computerization and automation is speed. A good database marketing system should ensure that the next stage of any sales cycle is accomplished more quickly and personally. If a customer asks for information, it should arrive quickly with a personalized letter. If the customer asks for a telephone call from a sales office or for a sales visit, these activities should be scheduled immediately. Even if we cannot fulfil the customer's expectations entirely (sales staff may be unavailable), we can ensure that an appropriate letter and additional information reach the customer quickly. Conversely, if it becomes clear that a customer should not be approached, this can be shown promptly on the database, to stop further approaches. The essence of contact strategy management is that we automate our response to our customers to achieve speed, but do it in a personalized way, so that customer satisfaction does not suffer.

Many media can be used in our contact strategy. These include:

- Telephone marketing: customer service/order taking, qualifying leads, appointment setting, response handling
- Direct mail: letters and various kinds of enclosure
- Inserts, catalogues and leaflets
- Electronic: telemessages, telex, fax, electronic mail, viewdata
- Press, TV and radio: support advertising, hand-raising, direct response
- Exhibitions: demonstrations, hand-raising
- Sales promotion: competitions, promotions
- The sales force: consultative selling, complex order taking
- Showrooms: demonstrations, confidence-building, customer education
- Seminars: customer education

In choosing the best contact strategy we take into account:

- Target customers – their nature and needs

- The messages we want to convey to our customers, and the role of each message in progressing our dialogue with them
- The media available. Their effectiveness varies not only with costs but also by product, target market and customer.

To determine our contact strategy, we build up a jigsaw from the strengths and weaknesses of each medium. Thus, if telephone is chosen as the prime medium but cannot deliver the required quantity of information, we can use mail as back-up, and the personalized follow-up pack should contain the information not communicable on the phone. However, the criteria we use to select media are only a guide, as we rely on controlled testing to finalize our choice. We do not test any medium in isolation, but in combination as part of a carefully defined contact strategy designed to be acceptable and credible to customers.

Enquiry management and fulfilment

We must be able to respond to customer needs at the time they are expressed. In database marketing, we call this enquiry management. When we receive a coupon, a telephone call, or a completed form from a customer, we must be able to deal with it quickly. When customers enquire about a product, their interest in it is usually more than transitory. The interest will not disappear if we do not respond instantly. But the customer may be making similar enquiries of our competition. If we respond quickly and appropriately (i.e. in a way that is right for the customer) we stand a better chance of making the sale. This is not just because we impress our customers with our professionalism, but also because if we present our 'case' first, it will have greater impact.

So, enquiry management is the pivot on which the success of a database marketing system turns. Even with the best database in the world, any database marketing system would fail without a good enquiry management system.

Initial management of enquiries

If a customer enquires by telephone, we must manage the enquiry initially by:

- Quickly extracting from the customer the information which enables us to decide which products or services he is interested in or are most suitable for him, now and in the future, and what the next step in managing the enquiry should be, taking into account the customer's expressed preferences concerning our response.
- Telling the customer what the next step will be.
- Implementing the next step quickly.

Subsequent management of enquiries

Very soon after the enquiry has been received, we must also be able to:

- Decide the remaining steps in handling the enquiry, based upon information derived from the enquiry and existing information on the database.
- Set in motion the mechanism which will deliver this strategy, including prioritization of enquiries.

The term fulfilment refers to the process by which the enquiry is managed to the point where the customer is satisfied with the conclusion. Fulfilment is part of the process of enquiry management. It may consist of a number of further steps, from sales visits, telephone calls, invitations to a retail shop, a sales seminar or exhibition, through to an order for the product. There are many different routes an enquiry can take. We may wish to deploy different types of response handling techniques, according to the type of customer and response. Fulfilment therefore requires clear and concise management.

The route to successful fulfilment is a clear contact strategy – a planned series of contacts with the customer aimed at gaining his commitment. This covers not just initial response, but a succession of responses, such as mailshots, telephone calls, invitations to events, and sales calls. A contact strategy is carefully planned and programmed. It is not left to the customer to call us back when he decides he wants to move to the next stage in his buying cycle. Nor is it left to the individual member of the supplier's staff – although every contact strategy must have some flexibility. A customer may enquire about one product, and then, while the sales cycle for that product is still in progress, enquire about another. Our recommended contact strategy might indicate a telephone call first, but if the salesman is calling about the first product, it makes sense for his call to deal with the second.

Product information and the enquiry

Product supply must be sufficient to meet the likely demand. If response exceeds available supply, customers are dissatisfied and sales are lost. If delay is inevitable, continuous contact (e.g by telephone) may help to maintain the customer's confidence that his order will be fulfilled.

Because we try to match products to needs, our database must contain product data. If we are in telephone contact with a customer, we should make accessible at a terminal a questionnaire which identifies which product is right for the caller, and then prompts the call receiver to ask questions to qualify the caller as a prospect. Our system should give information on product availability immediately. If we assume a product to be available, promise the customer early installation, and then fail to deliver on time, customer satisfaction will rapidly disappear.

Elements of the contact strategy

Database marketing can use any marketing communications medium or marketing channel as an element in its contact strategy, provided it is either addressable or it asks customers to identify themselves (hence the use of television to stimulate 'hand-raising' by potential customers). But together with the calling sales force, mail and telephone are the most highly addressable media and the ones most frequently used by database marketing companies.

The telephone

The telephone plays an important part in campaigns. Tollfree services are part of a rapidly growing trend. Customers are getting more used to being asked to call such numbers. The telephone is used in various ways in database marketing, including:

- As a tool in its own right, in telemarketing campaigns, where it is used to manage all relationships with the customer. Some companies now manage some of their customers entirely over the telephone, except for delivery of physical products and brochures. This has led to the emergence of the concept of telephone account management.
- As a back-up to other methods (e.g. to follow up responders or non-responders to a mail shot).
- As support to other elements of the marketing mix, such as the sales force, by screening leads, qualifying prospects or making appointments.
- To build a new list, or improve the quality of an existing list, by getting further information.
- To improve customer service (e.g by order taking, informing of progress, checking that product received or installed is satisfactory).
- To reactivate customers, by re-establishing a dialogue with those who have not bought for some time.
- Credit chasing.

The telephone is in daily use for most companies as a customer contact method. There is therefore a risk that database marketing disciplines will be overlooked when using the telephone as a marketing tool. If the telephone is used for our first contact with the customer, it may determine their impression of us for a long time. We must therefore get this contact right. The telephone is 'pressure sensitive' – too much pressure (when we cannot see the reactions on a customer's face) can lead to dramatic falls in productivity. Specialist training and management are therefore needed to ensure that telemarketing staff handle customers properly.

Telemarketing requires detailed planning. Whether or not we use a precise script or structure, each call must be under control and planned. Telemarketing differs from telephone selling in that every call is measured and the results analysed. This enables the different elements of telemarketing to be measured and tested as with direct mail – the list, the script, the offer, the timing and so on. Telemarketing also needs to be tested in competition with other media, and also with different combinations of media in the contact strategy.

The management of a telemarketing campaign must be very precise, including careful control of costs (e.g. operator time, list selection), through budgeting and planning of campaigns. Quality must be monitored particularly carefully. It is easy to target a telemarketing campaign to produce a specific number of appointments for the sales force, only to discover that the quality of appointments is very low. Telemarketing must therefore be measured as part of the overall contact strategy, which is designed to yield more sales and profit, not just appointments. The database must therefore be set up to allow tracking of the effectiveness of every contact medium from beginning to end of the sales cycle.

The difference between telemarketing as a database marketing medium, and telesales as practised in many companies, can be summarized as follows:

TELEMARKETING	TELEPHONE SELLING
Controlled message	Individual communication
– Uses structured scripts	– Operator's own methods
Variety of objectives	Objective to sell product or service
All results collected and analysed	Measurement haphazard – only sales
All parameters testable	Impossible to test elements
– List, offer, script, etc.	
Possible to plan and integrate with all other media	Usually stand-alone, with some mail follow-up
No commission usually paid	Commission paid, sometimes only commission

Compared with other database marketing media, telemarketing has the following strengths and weaknesses:

STRENGTHS	WEAKNESSES
Immediacy, high impact, personal contact	High unit cost per call (but low cost per customer and per sale if well targeted)
Two way medium	Risk of lack of commitment (verbal only)
– Interactive, active qualification	– Needs good follow up
– Information can be checked	
Flexible	Easily abused
– Variety of approaches	– Requires careful control
– Different scripts	– Pressure sensitive
– Answers questions/objections	

Accurate and controllable
– Easy to target
– Result from each call
– Testable in low volumes

Can optimize contact
– Selling up or across ranges
– Set appointments
– Update list during call
– Market feedback

Single dimension
– Voice only
– No pictures
– No written commitment

Must be effectively integrated
– With other marketing strategies
– Difficult to use in isolation

Direct mail

Direct mail has three main uses:

- As a prime medium – a self-contained vehicle for selling a product or service, promoting an event, etc.
- With other media, to support or follow up other activities.
- As support to a channel – before the sale (e.g. to provide leads) or after the sale (e.g. to follow up a sales call).

A direct mail campaign should follow the rules for using any database marketing medium laid out earlier. But each medium has its own way of achieving objectives. Consider some of the main questions of campaign design:

- To whom is the promotion directed? – In a mail campaign, unlike with telephone marketing and some other media, we cannot instantly adjust our response when interacting with the customer. We do not want to find out after the event whether the customer is the right one and whether the form of communication is right for him. Though the cost of each communication seems low, the costs of a large campaign are not. Misdirected mailshots waste print and postage and alienate customers. We therefore have to strike a balance between the suitability of a list and the cost of editing it. This is one reason why lists based on existing company data are usually the best – we have built them and should know their quality and appropriateness for each campaign.

- What do we want recipients to do? The direct mail package is the salesperson, a sales presentation and an order form, moving our relationship with the customer on (e.g. to receiving yet more information, accepting a sales visit, coming to our store, placing an order). We have to be very precise about what we want the customer to do.

- What will make the customer want to do it? Having set the objective, we must focus all our design effort on persuading the customer to do it. There will be no-one to help us when the letter arrives on the customer's desk or through his post box.

- How can we obtain customers' correct names and addresses? This depends on the quality of our database. If it is in the early stages of development, we may need to be very active in list development, mounting campaigns designed to move our relationship with customers forward and generate additional data.

- How much can we afford to pay for each sale or enquiry? For a mail test, we have to invest considerable sums, so much of our analysis must focus on the cost effectiveness of different approaches.

The letter

Most marketers are firm believers in the value of the letter to accompany any communication we are sending to customers. They see the letter in the following context:

The outer envelope	The knock on the door
The letter	The sales pitch
The brochure	The product or service demonstration
Samples and testimonials	Reassurance providers
Order form and reply envelope	The close

Just as one would never ask a salesperson simply to show his product without speaking, one should never send a brochure without a letter. However, some very successful campaigns have been without letters (or, for that matter, without brochures). There is of course no general rule except that what works, works, and we can only find that out by testing!

Letters are deceptively simple. Because we write letters often, we approach letter writing casually. The letter has fewer ways of attracting and retaining the reader's attention than other media. In a radio commercial, we can make noises, in a TV commercial, noises and movement, in the press or a leaflet, we can create 'multi-entry' communications (the prospect can start at any of various points, and does not need to read the whole leaflet). A salesman can see his prospect, and alter his pitch or tone according to the prospect's reactions. He can use his eyes, voice and body movements to compel attention and retain interest. But a letter has a good chance of being read, so effort invested in writing it brings rewards. All the rules for writing copy apply to letters, but there are many additional rules for letters which are too detailed to cover here.

The brochure

The brochure complements the letter. If the letter is the salesperson then the brochure is the product or service demonstration. The brochure should demonstrate the product or service, and turn the letter into pictures. If possible, the product should be shown yielding the benefits claimed for it. It should be supported by a full and logical story, guarantees and testimonials.

The catalogue

The well-used catalogue indicates a solid relationship with the customer. It is a permanent representative in the customer's office or home, selling all the year round without additional costs of following up. It also supports other channels. It can help the salesperson to sell the full range of products and services without having to explain them all. To achieve this, the catalogue must be a direct response vehicle – more than a listing of product, features and prices. It must create the desire to buy and be as readable and productive as any other piece of marketing material. The catalogue can be distributed in various ways – by mail, at exhibitions, handed out by sales staff, at shop counters, and so on.

Order forms

Order forms may be part of a brochure, catalogue or letter, whether separate or detachable. The order form is the salesperson's close, but the salesperson is not there, so it must make it as easy as possible. Typically it should look valuable, be reply paid, with the customer's details already entered and with clear instructions as to how to complete.

The envelope

It is the envelope which encourages the customer to take the step of seeing whether there is useful information contained in it. This usually means over-printing, and using paper of high quality appearance.

One piece mailers

One piece mailers are being used to reduce costs or to provide ways of giving more material to the customer within a cost budget. They may attract a low response, but this can be made up for by the higher coverage obtained within a given budget.

Enclosures

Many enclosures have been tried, with great success. They include gifts, testimonials, imaginative ways of showing the product in use, samples, guides or other items of enduring value.

Part II

MAKING IT HAPPEN

9 The database

In this chapter we consider some of the most important questions that relate to the development and management of the database:

- What is special about the information resources needed for database marketing?
- How do they differ from the data used in an analytical marketing system?
- What might the database contain, and why?
- How should the database be built?
- How should the data resource be managed?

On a technical note, this chapter makes no distinction between lists, files and database. The term database is used to describe any organized set of individual customer data, irrespective of their commercial or technical form.

Database characteristics

Information about customers and markets is one of the main assets of a marketing company. The information on a marketing database has to come from somewhere. Database marketing is 'learning by doing' – it provides most of the marketing information it needs. Each database marketing action uses information, but it also generates new information. This is because database marketing campaigns ask for responses. Each response contains information – at least, it should do. It is up to marketers to make sure that this information is of value. Thus, if a customer responds to an advertisement by calling a toll-free number, the questions the operator asks are designed not just to qualify the lead for the product or service which is the subject of the campaign. They should also provide information which will help in future campaigns.

In this way, database marketing builds up a store of information about individual customers. This information must be held in the most effective way. Unless it can be turned into profit, it is no use to us. The computer system is crucial for organizing the information and making it available. We must have clear objectives for computerising the data. The two main objectives are:

- To provide large volumes of segmented buyer and prospect data to help us develop profitable revenue streams through a data driven dialogue with the target audience
- To enable the marketing manager to analyse and segment the target audience in order to determine strategy.

We must be able to analyse and segment the database of buyers and enquirers, and to mobilize large volumes of segmented data for practical use in the variety of applications discussed in this book (e.g. lead generation and qualification, direct order fulfilment, direct mail, telemarketing). This is in marked contrast to the objectives of a conventional marketing information system, of which the typical objectives would be:

- To provide information enabling marketing management to monitor and forecast the performance of marketing mix elements (products, promotions, pricing, distribution channels) in different markets
- To provide information to help prioritize between markets for given products
- To help plan the allocation of marketing resources.

The applications usually built into a marketing information system include:

- Planning tools for long term forecasting, new product planning, annual sales and marketing planning
- Performance reports for different elements of the marketing mix, overall and by market sector
- Special audits of customer service.

To serve the above applications, the marketing information system requires mainly summary, aggregated or sample data, not individual customer data. The database marketer, on the other hand, needs information on the activity and characteristics of individual buyers and prospects.

Data design

Computers work best with information that is well organized to start with. That is why database marketing puts a strong emphasis on the structured collection of data. For example, telemarketing scripts must be designed to get the maximum amount of high quality information possible from customers, in a structured form. This allows the computer to take it without further intervention and add it to its database. The same applies to the design of forms to be completed by customers.

Structured information gathering is essential. Unless this discipline is observed from the beginning, problems will emerge later on. For example, the end of the financial year for companies is significant, either because they need to spend pre-allocated budgets, or because they are likely to be tightening their belts. We therefore may need to allocate space for that information in the computer, and collect it in a structured way.

The term database is used commonly in both computing and database marketing. A database is more than just raw data. It is data organized so that they can be used for their required purpose. A marketing database is a database that is built to be used for marketing purposes.

Given the many uses to which database marketing can be put and the many sectors in which it might be applied, there is no general formula stating exactly which data should be included in the database. Each database is tailored to the needs of its users. But it is important to avoid the mistake of designing it on the basis of past requirements.

The customer databases of many companies are not designed for marketing. They are more likely to be operations databases, used for order processing (order taking, delivery, invoicing, etc.) or after-sales service. They record what customers paid, and what they paid for, rather than helping to predict what they might like next!

The key to designing the database is to establish what data will be needed to facilitate capturing future revenue streams in the company's existing and future businesses. Many database marketing applications provide great opportunities for gathering data while marketing. The simplest example of this is the use of the questionnaire as part of the contact strategy. In summary, the data on the database must satisfy two criteria:

- They must be cost-effectively collectable
- They must be clearly required for future revenue stream generation

Sources of data

A database marketing system normally uses most of the customer information available within a company, but organizes it differently from the operations databases from which much of this customer information is likely to be drawn. Some new information will come from internal sources, such as the direct sales force. These proprietary data are one of a company's most valuable assets.

The word 'list' is common in database marketing. A list is the simplest form of marketing database. It is a set of names and how to contact them (e.g. addresses, telephone numbers). We use the word 'list' in two senses:

- A list which we purchase or rent for use in our campaigns or in building our own database. Clever list buying is the key to many successful database marketing campaigns.
- A list of target customers drawn from our database for a particular campaign. Careful list selection is the key to high response at low cost.

There are two types of data source, internal and external. Internal data include:

- Customer files
- Order records
- Service reports, complaints, etc.
- Merchandise return records
- Sales force records
- Application forms (e.g. for credit, insurance, promotional benefits)
- Market research
- Enquiries
- Warranty cards

External data include compiled and direct response lists from sources outside the company. Also included are classificatory data (e.g. census data and their derivations), which give ways of enhancing other external and internal data.

Data selection

The selection of data to include on the database is made according to the revenue stream and feasibility criteria mentioned above. Data should only be included if they help to answer questions such as these:

- Who are or will be my customers?
- Who do and will they buy from me or my competitors?
- Why do or will they maintain a dialogue with me?
- How can I retain them and increase their purchases from me?
- Where do I find others like them?
- When are they most receptive to buying from me?

If a data item does not help to answer these questions in a way that clearly leads to revenue defence and/or growth, then it should not be included. This obviously must take into account possible future revenue streams.

   In building the database, we cannot keep all the information we obtain about customers in the same way. Some data must be accessed quickly (e.g. data on customers who have recently received promotions). Other data can be accessible with a longer delay, and some might never be entered into the computer database. We must be careful about which data we do keep for quick access, or we will 'drown' the system with useless information. So another characteristic of database marketing systems is the constant check kept on which information is useful, and which data are 'nice to know', but not very useful.

Merging external data with proprietary data, or merging data from different proprietary sources, can be a problem. Special computer programs are normally used to do this. Problems arise when an individual or company is listed in different ways in different databases (or even in the same one). If the different databases are combined, customers may be listed more than once. We must get rid of this duplication, or deduplicate the list. Although we can computerizse much of this task, some human intervention may be necessary, as the computer can only deduplicate within certain tolerances. Depending on how important deduplication is, the computer may be asked to list entries where duplicate entry is suspected, for manual correction.

Data components

The types of information on the database may include:

- Customer or prospect i.e. information on how to access customers (e.g. address, telephone number) and on the nature and general behaviour of customers (psychographic and behavioural data).
- Transaction i.e. information on commercial transactions between the customer and the company e.g. orders, returns.
- Promotional i.e. information on what campaigns (tests and roll outs) have been launched, who has responded to them, what the final results have been in commercial and financial terms.
- Product i.e. information on which products have been involved in promotion, who has bought them, when and from where.
- Geodemographics i.e. information about the areas where customers live and the social or business category they belong to.

Customer data

The main design issue here is uniqueness. A customer must be uniquely identified, so that there is the minimum chance of confusion with another customer. But this must be done in an economical way, so as to reduce the space taken by the customer's record. To achieve this, some database designers use a match code (see p.98). If part of the database creation or updating process is deduplication, then the matchkey for each customer can be created at this stage. Many companies already have a unique coding system for their customers (e.g. credit card number, account number).

Many kinds of customer data might be included on the database. Examples for a consumer database include first name, last name, title, address (in meaningful format), sex, age, income, marital status, number of children, length of residence, whether recent or anticipated home mover, telephone number, special markers (VIP customer, do not promote, shareholder, frequent complainer), responses to questionnaires.

A business customer database might include company name, addresses of head office and relevant sites, telephone, fax and telex numbers, buyer's name, names of contacts and influencers, purchasing process, links with other companies, revenue and profits – size and growth, type of company (SIC code), number of employees, site structure, etc.

People with like interests and similar purchasing patterns tend to live in similar areas. Geodemographic data can therefore add a useful dimension to the customer profile. Coding schemes such as ACORN, PINPOINT and MOSAIC are used to categorize consumers who live in particular areas. This method is widely used, but it does have some limitations, as shown in Figures 9.1 and 9.2.

Transaction data

Past transactions are one of the most important indicators of likely future transactions. The use of FRAC (Frequency, Recency, Amount and Category) in direct marketing is based on years of experience of finding that these variables dominate most explanations of buying behaviour for existing products. This means that the transaction data must include information which allows FRAC information to be extracted on a customer basis. This means that the details of each purchase for each customer must be logged. This includes not only the obvious 'identifying' details (who bought or returned what, when, how, etc.), but also the associated marketing data (at what price, from which promotion).

As Figure 9.2 shows, in consumer markets, transaction data can be much more effective as a basis for selection than geodemographic variables, where we are trying to establish the needs of existing customers in relation to a new product. However, the widespread availability of geodemographic data which are matchable to individual customer data is changing this situation. A company with limited or no transaction data available can start with a campaign based mainly on geodemographic data which will normally be organized in a national file based on the electoral roll enhanced with postal coding and possibly telephone numbers. Census information will usually be used to enhance the file further and provide some of the basis for demographic classification. This can create problems of matching addresses to census information. If any internal or research data specific to a company's market are available to assist in developing a profile of prospective users, this can be used to create a 'scoring module' or 'directory' for selecting target customers from the national file. Similar arguments apply to publicly available databases on business markets.

The campaign should create transaction data fairly quickly, while the geodemographic data may continue to be useful in segmentation and selection. The emergence of companies offering comprehensive data services (list validation,

Figure 9.1: Selecting prospects using geographic data

Figure 9.2: Selecting prospects using purchasing data and scoring

data pooling, matching to other files) means that very few new users of database marketing will be entirely devoid of relevant data.

Product data

In a one product company, this raises no problem – each transaction is either a sale or a return. In companies with very wide product ranges, product classification may be problematic, and a numbering system to suit the requirements of database marketing may have to be adopted. Such a system must allow like products to be grouped easily.

Promotion data

Documentation of past and present promotions in some detail (right down to which customers were subject to them, and the media and contact strategy used) is essential if the effectiveness of promotions is to be measured and if promotional planning is to benefit from analysis of the past.

Data quality

Data do not stay fresh, but become stale, as the contact on which they were based recedes into the past. We know this only too well from looking at population census data in areas of high mobility. The same may apply to purchasing authorities in large companies. So we occasionally have to carry out special exercises to check the validity of data and/or update them. This maintenance of the database is very important.

The quality of the data drawn from a database depends mainly on: how up to date the source data are; and whether they contain the detail needed to access the right individuals (names, addresses, telephone numbers, job titles). The quality of the data is measured by results of the last audit carried out on them. It should be possible to carry out some quality checks via testing.

Merging databases and purging them of errors and duplicates saves costs and prevents customers being alienated by being contacted more than once with the same objective. Deduplication of many items may need to be undertaken, so merging and purging of large databases requires sophisticated computer software. This process is easier if:

- All data are entered in standard format
- Matching rules are used which recognize duplicates
- Efficient fulfilment procedures exist, so that all transactions are recorded and customers are helped to signal any duplicates or errors

- Different ways of selecting customers are available
- Auditing procedures exist.

Databases get out of date quickly. People change addresses and jobs. Companies move, new companies are set up and companies go out of existence. Errors in fulfilment records occur, through commission and omission. This is why audits must be undertaken. Questionnaire mailing can be an effective but costly way of improving data quality.

The quality of information also depends on customer-contact staff (sales, telemarketing, retail branch, etc.) understanding the value of high quality information and the importance of their feedback in improving its quality. Every opportunity must be used to improve data quality, during every contact with the customer – with sales staff, over the telephone, in showrooms and dealer outlets, on service calls, in shops and at exhibitions, by return of guarantees, via competitions and through past customer records. Lists can be traded with relevant businesses to help here. But the advantage of using our own database is that it consists of people who have done and are doing business with us, trust us and will therefore respond better to us.

External lists are often classified into mail responsive and compiled. Mail responsive lists consist of anyone who uses the post for transactions which could be carried out in some other way e.g. mail order customers. Compiled lists are those compiled to cover particular kinds of people (e.g. conference attendees, product buyers, small businesses). Lists can be sourced from list brokers who often act as agents for list owners. They may also be sourced from directories and by research.

Techniques for merging and purging data

The second group of specialist techniques used in database marketing relate to managing the information flowing from different sources so that the resulting merged data are of high quality e.g. with no duplicates or spelling errors. The need for good quality data has led to the development of computerized systems for identifying duplicates and errors and correcting them automatically or semi-automatically. Software is available to carry out the following:

- The filing of all customers and prospects together with their relevant data (e.g. type and date of purchasing activity).
- Merging of bought or rented lists with in-house lists.
- Identification and purging of duplicates.
- Matching and merging of data which relate to the same customer.
- Postcoding of addresses, for ease of access to census data, accuracy of targeting and easier sorting for postal rebates.
- Validation of names against relevant official or national standard files, or

telephone company directories, to ensure that prospective customers are actually resident at the stated address.

At the heart of such software lies its matching technique. The approach used usually depends on whether consumer or business customers are the focus. The first and most important characteristic of the software is which variables it uses to match. Here are some examples of match definition:

CONSUMER	BUSINESS
• Individual at an address	• Individual with a company
• Surname at an address	• Job title with company
• Household delivery contact point	• Company at an address
	• Company name at any address

No database is perfect – even supposedly 'national standard' ones – so the actual level of match achieved can vary tremendously. The twin objectives of maximizing the level of match (i.e. the proportion of matches which are successful) while maintaining the accuracy of the match will often be in conflict. The higher the level of match required, the more likely it is that manual correction will be needed. The level of match for consumer data may often be in the range 70–95 per cent. But the level of match for business data is often much lower. This is mainly because of the many variations in data formats used by different industrial data sources, compared to consumer data sources, which usually only vary by the different ways there are of representing name and address. Since consumer addresses are on average shorter and simpler than business ones, there is less likelihood of simple errors (e.g. transposition of numbers).

The software to do all this goes beyond the simple match code, using complex decision trees and mathematical scoring formulae to simulate human judgement.

What is a duplicate?

This is the first question to be addressed in every merge/purge. The specific definition will vary according to the database marketer's needs and the capabilities of the software being used. The software must identify, for pairs of names and addresses, which pairs are duplicates and which represent separate individuals.

Pair 1	J.Roberts 46 Cranbrook Road London W4 2LH	J.Roberts 46 Cranbrook Road London W4 2LH
Pair 2	Bob Shaw 46 Cranbrook Road London W4 2LH	Dr K.R.Shaw, 1 Surrey Street London WC2R 2PS

It appears obvious that the first pair is the duplicate and the second two different individuals. In fact, the second pair is the duplicate. The first pair are a brother Jim staying with his sister Jean; the second a private name address and a work name and address for the same person. There is no way to pick up these kinds of duplicate except by contacting every name on a list. In other words, there is no economically reasonable way of achieving a list which is guaranteed completely free of duplicates.

Because matching requires a large amount of computer memory, a match code may be created by the software to represent a customer. The match code is an abbreviated form of the address. An example of a 14 digit match code derived from a name and address is as follows:

ADDRESS	ITEM FROM WHICH CODE	VALUE TAKEN
Addison Lee	Outward postcode	WC2N
45–64 Chandos Place	Number of characters in name	7
London	Name (1st, 3rd, 4th)	ADI
WC2N 4HS	Number (1st, 2nd, 3rd)	45–
	Street (1st, 3rd, 4th)	CAN
Derived match code		WC2N 7 ADI 45–CAN

Further examples of computerized matching are shown in Figure 9.3. This is adapted from an actual merge/purge procedure, and shows how matches of names and addresses on two lists are displayed.

COMPANY NAME	ADDRESS LINE 1	ADDRESS LINE 2	ADDRESS LINE 3
Jones Assoc.	3 West Street	Coventry	CV4 8AR
Jones Associates	3 West St.	Coventry	CV4 8AR
Jones (Fred) Assoc.	West Street	Earlsdon	Coventry
Jonesco	Vine Street	Cardiff	CF9 5PQ
Jonesco	Vine Street	Cardiff	CF9 5PQ
Jot-it Ltd	Sussex Street	Croydon	CR12 4DT
Jot-it & Co. Ltd.	2 Sussex Street	Croydon	CR12 4DT

Figure 9.3: Example of computerized matching: duplicate address report

Quality validation of merging and purging

The ability of merging and purging software to carry out its job is so important to building a quality database that special tests have been developed to assess this ability. These tests must be comprehensive, as the merge/purge software may be used to combine records from many sources. These sources include in-house lists, rented and bought third party lists and suppression lists (lists used to eliminate records of certain customers – such as those with bad debt histories, or 'nixies' – customers who do not exist at the address stated, perhaps because they have died or gone away).

There are four steps to a merge/purge:

- Conversion to a standard format. During this step, unwanted or invalid characters and records are usually deleted, postal codes are corrected, and standard data items (e.g. sex, job function, home address for business customer) are coded
- Deduplication, in which various tests are applied to identify duplicates
- Split and key, in which the deduplicated and cleaned output is grouped into the type of records required for the list, and key codes are applied to each list
- Pre-sort, in which the records are sorted to aid exploitation of postal discounts.

Because of the number of ways in which a customer's details may appear in different list sources, the conversion to standard format is a critical part of the merge/purge process.

Database marketing users who are considering acquiring merge/purge software, or hiring an agency to do the job for them, should test the quality of different offerings by providing carefully structured sample lists of the kind to be used, with known occurrences of the problems requiring solution (e.g. spelling errors, omission of spaces, use of aliases, multiple names at an address, different forms of names, mispunctuation, and so forth). This will reveal which software or service performs best for the kinds of lists likely to be used by the customer. Scoring systems have been devised to measure the success of different software packages in carrying out the task. These systems take into account partial solutions of problems. However, it is not enough to simply achieve deduplication, as users have many other requirements of merge/purge software. These include:

- The ability of the software to follow detailed, different instructions, to carry out various counts (e.g. how many of certain kinds of cases deleted, overall and from different lists) and to produce a variety of reports on the outcomes of its application
- Net output statistics (how many names are available to market to).

Most database marketers agree that substantial investment in merge/purge software is often required to set up a useful database. But the investment is well worth while, and pays considerable dividends in terms of reduced marketing costs, increased revenue and enhanced customer satisfaction.

Using the database

A database designed and used for database marketing may be a company's best marketing database of any kind and of great value to all marketing and sales staff. Sales staff will use it for journey planning, marketing staff for marketing planning. Retail site planners will use it for making site decisions. The database starts from the individual customer and is gradually built up. This contrasts with some marketing and sales databases which deal in aggregates – they identify business potential within an area, but without identifying the potential business available from individual customers.

We can use our database to track the responses coming from an individual customer. Each customer or prospect has a history of contact with us. This information is often lost. This has two consequences:

1. We may approach the same customer in successive days (or worse, on the same day) with different messages (or the same message delivered twice). This cannot be avoided – a customer may read an advertisement and receive a mail shot on the same day. But we can minimize the wastefulness of such events by ensuring that we coordinate our different direct approaches.
2. Without a history, we may lose our flag or marker as to where the customer is in his 'buying cycle'. This tells us when it is appropriate to telephone or schedule a sales visit.

The database gives us a measure of our success in moving a prospect through a sales cycle. This is of great value to sales staff. For example, we could ask for a list of customers in a particular market sector with a particular product who have not responded to our last mail shot on the subject. These could either be followed up more forcefully (e.g. by telephone), or (if there were other priorities) be omitted from a telephone prospecting campaign, because lack of response (perhaps after second mailing) demonstrated lack of interest.

The history of our relationship with customers can be used to calculate the costs and benefits of acquiring particular kinds of customers, not just in terms of the first sale that we make to them, but over the life of our relationship with them. For example, if our database shows that customers who buy product X are 50 per cent more likely to buy product Y than other customers, then the benefits of acquiring a customer for X extend beyond the profit that we make on X. This enables us to take a more comprehensive view on the viability of particular campaigns.

With a full history of our marketing relationship with customers, we can use the database to identify customers most likely to respond positively when we market to them. This is because we have enough information to identify our success in selling to different groups of customers. When we identify that a customer is a member of a particular group, we assume he has the same likelihood as other members of the group to buy a particular product. In its most advanced form, this process emerges as 'scoring'. The score that we give a customer in relation to a given product is determined by:

- Our analysis of all his characteristics
- Our assessment as to whether those characteristics, when they appear in whole groups of customers, make those customers likely to buy.

Once we have identifed which characteristics are important, we can devise a scoring method which can be applied instantly, by the computer. This score indicates the likelihood that the customer will buy. This information is combined with campaign objectives to determine a priority for the response.

10 Technical management

Several technical factors must be taken into account in designing and managing the database and the system which creates and applies it. The evolution of computing technology must be considered, as database marketing requires a substantial investment in hardware and software. Figures 10.1 and 10.2 illustrate some of the main components of a modern computer installation. Before investing in the development of such a system, the following questions need to be answered:

- Is the investment sound?
- If a system is purchased which meets the company's immediate needs, what happens when these needs change? Will the software have to be rewritten? Will a larger processor or much more storage be required?
- Will the system be able to communicate with any piece of hardware from any manufacturer likely to be supplying systems with which the database marketing system will have to interface?
- Can the supplier chosen deliver the highest standards of reliability, service and support? Does he have the full range of required products?

Hardware

When the first general purpose computer was built in the mid 1940s, it contained 18,000 vacuum tubes, weighed five tons, occupied six rooms and could process 10,000 instructions per second. It cost $5m to build. Today, more processing power is available on a piece of silicon 5mm square and 0.5mm thick, costing less than $5 in a local electronics store. This rate of advance is continuing

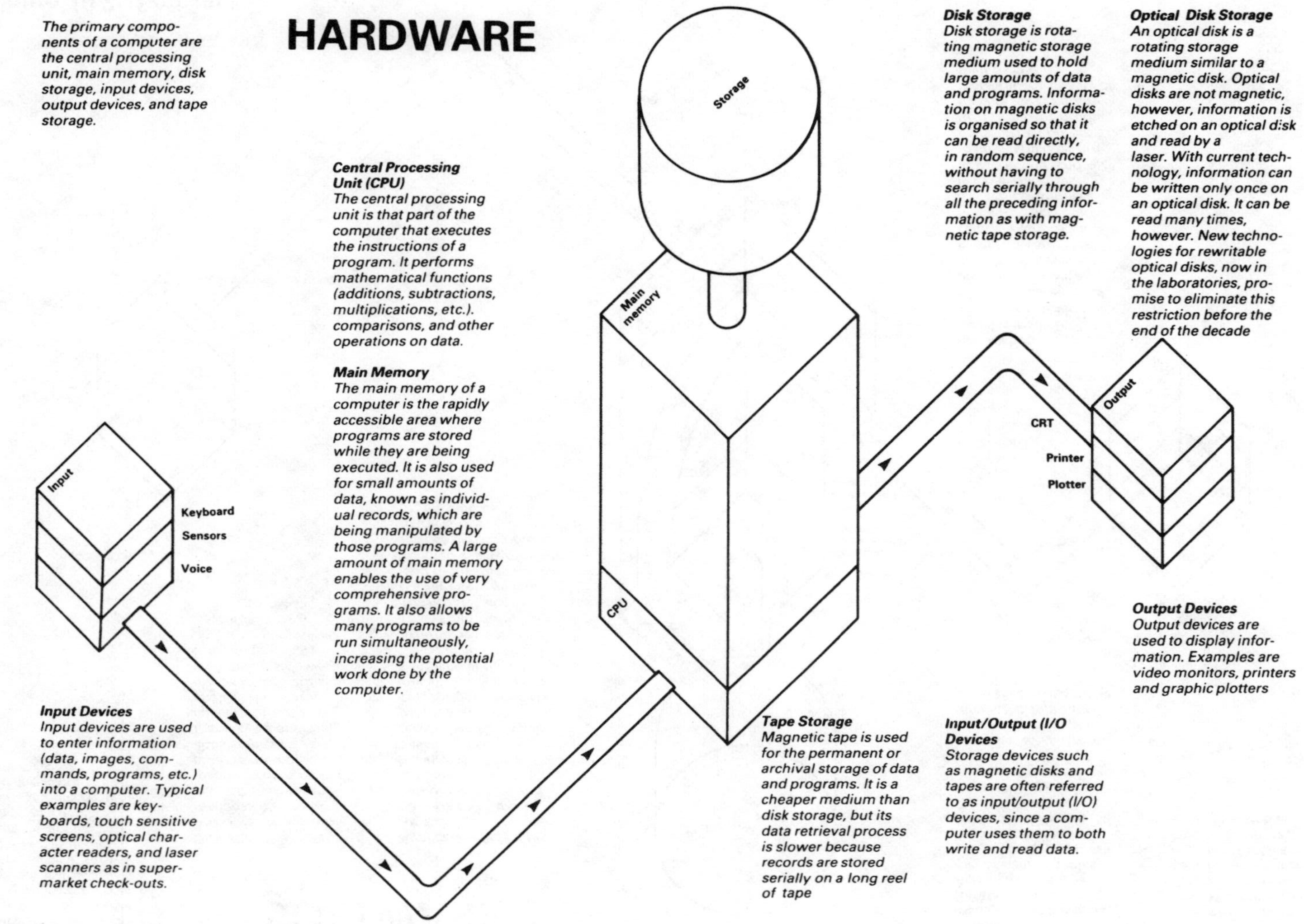

HARDWARE

The primary components of a computer are the central processing unit, main memory, disk storage, input devices, and tape storage.

Central Processing Unit (CPU)
The central processing unit is that part of the computer that executes the instructions of a program. It performs mathematical functions (additions, subtractions, multiplications, etc.), comparisons, and other operations on data.

Main Memory
The main memory of a computer is the rapidly accessible area where programs are stored while they are being executed. It is also used for small amounts of data, known as individual records, which are being manipulated by those programs. A large amount of main memory enables the use of very comprehensive programs. It also allows many programs to be run simultaneously, increasing the potential work done by the computer.

Input Devices
Input devices are used to enter information (data, images, commands, programs, etc.) into a computer. Typical examples are keyboards, touch sensitive screens, optical character readers, and laser scanners as in supermarket check-outs.

Keyboard
Sensors
Voice

Input

Disk Storage
Disk storage is rotating magnetic storage medium used to hold large amounts of data and programs. Information on magnetic disks is organised so that it can be read directly, in random sequence, without having to search serially through all the preceding information as with magnetic tape storage.

Optical Disk Storage
An optical disk is a rotating storage medium similar to a magnetic disk. Optical disks are not magnetic, however, information is etched on an optical disk and read by a laser. With current technology, information can be written only once on an optical disk. It can be read many times, however. New technologies for rewritable optical disks, now in the laboratories, promise to eliminate this restriction before the end of the decade

Output Devices
Output devices are used to display information. Examples are video monitors, printers and graphic plotters

Input/Output (I/O) Devices
Storage devices such as magnetic disks and tapes are often referred to as input/output (I/O) devices, since a computer uses them to both write and read data.

Tape Storage
Magnetic tape is used for the permanent or archival storage of data and programs. It is a cheaper medium than disk storage, but its data retrieval process is slower because records are stored serially on a long reel of tape

Storage

Main memory

CPU

Output

CRT
Printer
Plotter

Figure 10.1: Hardware

SOFTWARE

Software is the generic term used to describe computer programs in general. There are many types of software, including operating systems, application programs, database management systems, and application development tools.

Operating Systems
An operating system manages the computer. It allocates the resources of the computer to the various application programs that may be operating concurrently. It also enables those programs to communicate with the outside world through terminals and other peripheral devices.

Application Programs
An application program performs a business task or other function in support of some external events such as payroll or accounts receivable. Application programs may be custom-developed specifically for one user or company or they may be supplied by an external vendor in a "packaged" form. These application packages are generalised so that they can be adapted easily, through the use of parameters, to the needs of different organisations.

Database Management Systems (DBMS)
A database management system enables an application program to store data on disk and retrieve it easily. The DBMS will also enable the application program to retrieve related records. For example, when dealing with a specific customer, the application program can use the DBMS to retrieve all orders for that customer only. Without a DBMS, the program would have to know the order number of each specific order before it could be retrieved.

Application Development Tools
There is an important additional category of programs known as application development software. This category embraces many products that assist programmers in developing, testing, documenting, and maintaining their programs. Their purpose is to improve the productivity of the programmers and the quality of their programs.

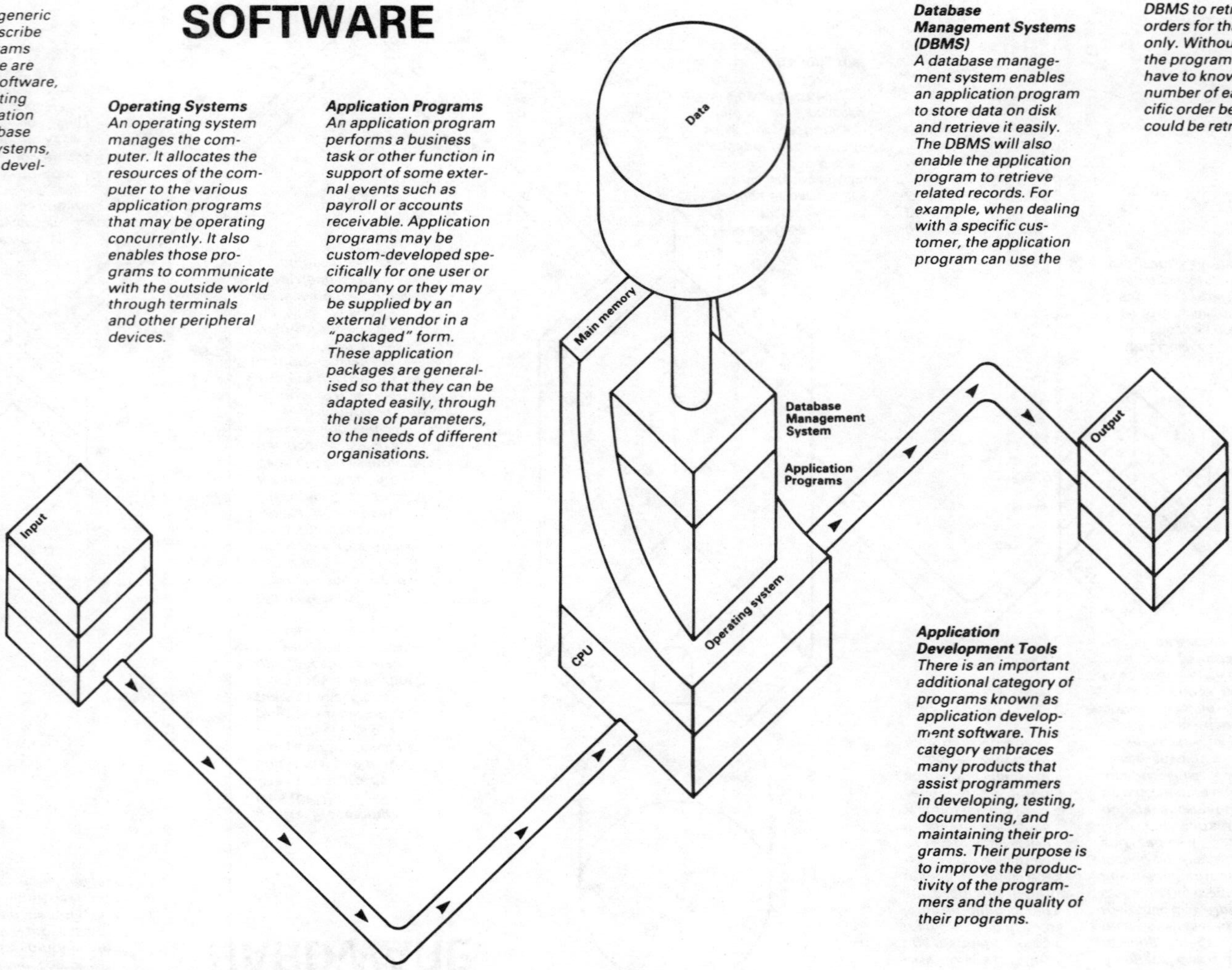

Data

Main memory

Database Management System

Application Programs

Operating system

CPU

Input

Output

Figure 10.2: Software

unabated. Circuitry is improving about 20 per cent each year in price performance. The size of a given circuit is falling by about 30 per cent each year.

Mainframes and microcomputers

The idea that the mainframe is becoming obsolete is very far from the truth
when it comes to the handling of very large databases. The mainframe is alive
and well, performing data management functions at the heart of the majority of
the information systems of most large organizations. The amount of mainframe
processing capacity is still increasing very fast.

Although the cost of mainframe processing is falling by 20 per cent each year,
it is becoming increasingly difficult for mainframe manufacturers to stretch the
limits of technology encountered by the very largest systems. Fundamental
natural laws, such as the speed of light and the ability of silicon to dissipate
heat, introduce severe problems as the speed of chips and the number of circuits
on them increase. As a result, the speed of the fastest mainframes is increasing
at only (!) 15 per cent each year.

This limitation can significantly affect the plans of those very large users who
are already operating the largest machines available and whose needs are
growing fast. They must plan on distributing their processing load across a
network of machines managing multiple databases. They may use increasingly
complex combinations of mainframes, minicomputers and microcomputers to
reduce the burden on the mainframe, by more distributed processing.

Micro and minicomputers

The main advantage of microcomputers is that they are very cheap. Although
a relatively small outlay will acquire quite a powerful machine, there are significant limitations to what can be achieved with microcomputers. Their internal
speeds are slow in comparison with mainframes, making certain database
marketing requirements, such as sorting, rather time consuming, and absorbing
all a machine's processing capacity so that it will not be usable for anything else
while it is processing. Minicomputers are of course a half way house in this
respect. But for the very largest databases, the use of one (or more) mainframes
will be essential.

Storage

Technology for storing data is one of the limiting factors in database marketing,
which is characterized by very large databases, frequently accessed and changed.
Once, when database marketing systems were off-line, and batch processing
was used, tape storage devices were the main storage medium. With competitive
pressures forcing companies to reach higher marketing standards, the need is
for systems which can access and alter information on-line (e.g. while the

customer is on the other end of the line – whether it be a telephone or a data line). This demands the use of disk storage. Disk storage has been falling in cost about 20 per cent each year, but its performance has not improved so radically. Disk storage devices are basically electromechanical, and this imposes limitations on how far their speed can be increased. So the time taken to find and retrieve data has not improved dramatically. This will be a limiting factor in the design of database marketing systems for years to come.

External bureaux

An option open to a company which is reluctant to acquire a mainframe and the staff to operate it is to use commercial bureaux. These provide mainframe time on a service basis. Today, there is a wide choice of companies offering this service. Advances in telecommunications have made the location of the mainframe almost irrelevant – in some cases, mainframe and user company may be separated by oceans. Until the advent of micro and minicomputers, these bureaux provided the main route for companies taking their first steps in database marketing. Today, they still perform this function for many companies, providing a quick and relatively trouble free way to start.

Database management systems

A database management system (DBMS) is a software system that enables application programs to store data and retrieve them easily. The relationship of a DBMS to other software on a computer installation is shown in Figure 10.2. In particular, a DBMS enables an application program to store and retrieve related data records. Related records are those that share a common characteristic, for example, records that represent orders for a given customer, or records that represent customers who have received a particular mail shot. Many types of application program tend to retrieve records based on relationships. For example, a selection for a campaign for product X might require the computer to select all those customers who purchased product Y from us within the last five years.

The DBMS must adopt a method of representing these relationships and retrieving records based on them. How these relationships are implemented in software is the main way in which different types of DBMS are classified. The three main types of DBMS are:

- Relational
- Hierarchical
- Network

Figure 10.3 illustrates these categories and explains them in brief.

DATABASE MANAGEMENT SYSTEMS

A database management system (DBMS) has been described previously as a software system that enables application programs to store data and retrieve it easily. In particular, a DBMS enables an application program to store and retrieve related data records.

Related records are those that share a common characteristic, for example records that represent different orders for the same customer. Since application programs tend to retrieve records based on those relationships ("Find all the orders for size 10 widgets for the ABC Company"), the database management system must adopt a method of representing these relationships and retrieving records based on them. The manner in which the relationships are implemented is the primary characteristic by which DBMSs are categorized.

The three primary categories of DBMS are relational, hierarchical, and network.

Relational DBMS

Assume that customer orders for products must be represented in a database. The records representing them would appear as shown below in a relational database.

This data representation is quite simple and easy to comprehend. Each type of record is represented as existing in a table or file of like records. It is also intuitively obvious to the user what types of relationships are implemented and how they can be manipulated. For instance, one could easily determine the names of all the customers who had ordered washers – part number P3 – by searching the order file for all line items containing the product number P3 and then searching the customer file for all the customes with the same numbers as those in the records extracted from the order file.

The essential advantages of a relational database are its simplicity and flexibility. A relational database can be used to extract information on the basis of whatever relationships are represented by data in the tables.

Hierarchical DBMS

In a hierarchical database, records are represented as having "owners". In a pure hierarchical database, each record may have one owner, whereas an owner record may own many "members".

Continuing with the previous example, the records for SMITH's orders would appear as shown below.

The customer record "owns" two "members" – the order records. Note that the customer number is no longer included in the order record. It is replaced by two different types of links (the arrows), one vertical linking the customer record to the first order and the other (horizontal) linking orders for the same customer together. Similar records would exist for the orders for the other customers.

Network DBMS

The network DBMS overcomes the one-owner-per-member limitation by introducing additional record types. Continuing the previous example, SMITH's orders would be represented as indicated below in a network system:

The notable differences are that the product identity has disappeared from the order record and is replaced by a linkage that connects all orders for a given product. Thus, each order record has two linkages, one to relate it to the customer and one to relate it to the product. As with the hierarchical system, the entities to which the order is related are not obvious from its data content. The user must know what linkages have been established in order to know on what basis data can be retrieved.

A problem arises in attempting to relate the order records to the products. If, for example, all orders containing product P3 were being sought, then either links from the product record for P3 to all such orders would be necessary (violating the one-owner-per-member rule) or all order records would have to be able to be searched. There are ways around these difficulties but they introduce complexities to a purely hierarchical system and are not as intuitively obvious as with the relational approach.

Summary

The relative simplicity of the relational DBMS makes it suitable for manipulation by non-data processing personnel. This type of database management system therefore provides a desirable foundation on which to base analytic applications developed by end users. On the other hand, data processing specialists will recognize the potentially poor performance of a relational system if its needs to search through a large number of records. The linkage-based systems, however, can be designed for good performance by a suitable choice of linkages. Linkage-based systems do require that the user know what relationships have been implemented and, to some extent, how they have been implemented. Consequently, use of these systems tends to be restricted to information systems specialists.

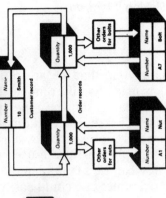

Customer records

Number	Name
10	Smith
30	Jones
45	Brown
80	Black

Product records

Number	Name
A1	Nut
A7	Bolt
P3	Washer

Order records

Customer number	Product number	Quality
10	A1	1,000
10	A7	1,000
30	P3	500
45	A1	2,000
45	A7	1,000
45	P3	3,000
80	A1	600
80	A7	200
80	P3	200

Customer record

Number	Name
10	Smith

Order records

Number	Quantity
A1	1000

Number	Quantity
A7	1000

Figure 10.3: Database management systems

Relational

Let us assume that we are representing the number of purchases of different products made by different customers. The records representing these purchases would appear as shown in the appropriate columns of Figure 10.3 in a relational database. This representation of the data is quite easy to understand. Each type of record is represented as existing in a table or file of like records. It is also intuitively obvious to the user what types of relationship are implemented and how they can be manipulated.

For example, one could easily find the names of all customers who had bought life insurance by searching the purchases record for all lines containing products with policy numbers representing life insurance, and then searching the customer record for all the customers with the same numbers as those extracted from the purchases record.

The main advantages of a relational database are its simplicity and flexibility. A relational database can be used to extract information on the basis of whatever relationships are represented by data in the tables. The actual location of the data does not matter. The required data emerge through 'logical sifting', and the user is insulated from the physical structure of the database. The sifting is done by a computer language called a query language. There are several of these, but the commonest by far is SQL (structured query language), which came orginally from IBM. It can join tables together and break them apart to look at the data from different angles.

Hierarchical

In a hierarchical database, records are represented as having 'owners'. In a pure hierarchical database, each record may have one owner, whereas an owner record may have many 'members'. Using the same example as above, the record for Smith's purchases would appear as shown in the appropriate columns of Figure 10.3. The customer record 'owns' two 'members' – the purchase records. Note that the customer number is no longer included in the purchase record. It is replaced by two different kinds of link (the arrows). One links the customer record to the first purchase and the second links all purchases from the same customer together. Similar records would exist for all other customers.

Using this approach, a problem arises in attempting to relate the purchase records to the products. If, for example, all purchases containing product P3 were being sought, then either links from the product record for P3 to all such purchases would be necessary (violating the one owner per member rule) or all order records would have to be searched. There are various ways around these difficulties, but they create complexities in a purely hierarchical system and are not as intuitively obvious as with the relational approach.

To write applications software for a hierarchical database, one must understand the database's physical layout because programs have to find their way through the database to where the data is stored.

Network

The network database overcomes the one owner per member limitation by introducing additional record types. Smith's purchases would be represented as indicated in the appropriate columns of Figure 10.3 in a network system.

The main differences are that the product identity has disappeared from the purchase record and is replaced by a linkage that connects all purchases of a given product. Thus, each purchase record has two linkages, one to the customer and one to the product type. As with the hierarchical system, the entities to which the purchase is related are not obvious from its data content. The user must know what linkages have been established in order to know on what basis data can be retrieved.

DBMS summary

The simplicity of a relational DBMS makes it suitable for manipulation by less specialist staff. It is therefore ideal as a foundation for basing applications which are developed by end users. On the other hand, performance may be poor if the system needs to search through a large number of records. The linkage-based systems can be designed for good performance by specifying those linkages which are most likely to be needed in an application. Users of linkage-based systems need to know what linkages have been implemented and perhaps even how they have been implemented. For this reason, use of these systems tends to be restricted to information systems specialists.

DBMS software has been developed to aid all data management, not just database marketing. Typically, a database marketing system would be developed using one of the many DBMS packages available. Until recently, a DBMS was an isolated product that enabled systems developers to relate data items to each other for easier retrieval. In recent years, choice of DBMS software has emerged as a strategic choice for the user. It can dictate the choice of many other systems development tools. Choice of DBMS can limit the applications packages that can be used, as not all applications packages work with all DBMS packages. For this reason, a business dependent on one or more central databases (whether financial, marketing or in any other function) must develop a strategic information system plan, with future applications needs clearly identified, before choosing its DBMS package.

Productivity

Because of the high software costs of most database marketing systems, marketing management needs to maintain a balance between the technical effectiveness of the system and the costs of developing and running it.

Some DBMS suppliers also supply an integrated set of development aids and program management tools. These are aimed at increasing the productivity of systems development. These proprietary tools use a central data dictionary that stores technical definitions of all the data in the database, the transactions applied to the data, the reports and screen displays to be generated, and the nature of the various processes that are used to manipulate and maintain the data. These tools include program generators for transactions and reports, system testing tools, on-line query capabilities, and more advanced languages for end-users to modify and design applications.

Measuring the productivity of systems development is a complicated and controversial task. Numerous analytical techniques have been developed, but none have proved to be acceptable to all, although all systems managers agree on the need for increased development productivity.

Unfortunately, while the costs of hardware have declined dramatically in recent years, the cost of skilled computing staff has risen almost as fast. With companies demanding highly customised systems, database development has become a labour intensive function.

The performance of the computer system is measured in terms of the time (and hence cost) of performing a given set of instructions. The time is taken by two main activities – storing and retrieving data (essentially the time taken by the data retrieval arm in the disk pack – known as Input/Output or I/O time) and the time taken performing instructions (known as Central Processing Unit or CPU time). The performance of the database developed using the DBMS package chosen is measured in terms of how much computer power it takes. This is a function of two factors, the physical design of the database and the inherent performance of the chosen DBMS.

Given the above factors, the challenge facing management is to plan its database development investment and manage it appropriately, while both marketing and systems worlds are changing rapidly.

Managing the data resource

The unplanned or ill-conceived deployment of a company's data resource wastes time and money. It can also competitively disadvantage the company. Effective database management is a skilled task, which is why in the traditional direct marketing industry there is a trend towards list management. This means that a third party takes over the management of a company's marketing database, whether for rental or the company's own use. The need for specialist skills in managing large databases is being recognized by the appointment of database administrators. In the marketing department, we may one day see the marketing database manager, who will perform tasks such as:

- Taking responsibility for collection, consolidation and storage of data from other corporate databases and other sources
- Taking responsibility for the quality of data
- Being responsible for traffic control
- Processing requests for database access
- Managing contacts with data users
- Providing users with detailed activity and cost reports.

The database is unlikely to be part of a larger integrated corporate database, for the foreseeable future. The very high volume batch access to a database marketing system suggests that it may be better to keep it separate from other corporate databases. This may be needed for security reasons, given the high commercial value and possible sensitivity of the data.

To guarantee the quality of the database, the database manager must make sure that all records are entered in a standard format, that matching rules are used to identify duplicates, and that duplicates are merged and purged in an agreed way. Definition of duplicates is complex, as we have already seen. Affinities between records (e.g. employees of the same company or family) may need to be known when planning a contact strategy. Ideally, any affinities should be entered at source, but this means training data entry staff or possibly changing source data systems. Both are major undertakings, so all too often the task of identifying affinities is left until after most customer records have been entered. Data management staff are left with the problem.

Planning, designing and implementing the database

Marketing databases often do not meet database marketers' needs. This can frustrate senior management, who may complain that:

- Too much money is spent on the database
- Too many projects are planned
- Data are already proliferating throughout the organization
- Performance of the computer in retrieving data is not as cost-effective as promised
- New data requirements cannot be met from existing source systems, resulting in a patchwork of enhancements to many existing systems to provide the database marketer with what he needs.

These problems can only be overcome through better planning, design and implementation.

Planning

During the planning stage, success depends upon the following factors:

- A clear vision of future applications and the revenue streams that will flow from them, and in what period. This will define the boundaries of the database, and make clear what management's objectives are.
- Integration with mainstream systems planning activities. The database marketing system will interface with many other corporate systems, taking data from them and returning data to them. So the development and operation of the database marketing system must be unified with that of other corporate systems.
- Creativity of the planning team. Planning team members need a combination of business, analytical, technical and communication skills. Project team members must know enough about the company's business to discuss objectives with senior management, and hardware and software strategies with data processing personnel. The team must include very skilled marketing staff, with the vision to identify future revenue sources and possible sources of relevant data. Techniques to stimulate creativity may need to be used frequently for this part of the project.
- Data design expertise. This is needed not just for the main database, but also for determining how data is to be used by the main applications.

Design

The design of the database starts with the 'logical' data design. This is often produced by 'data modelling', a technique used to define what data are needed, their meaning and the relationship between data items. A data model is a diagram showing what data are collected and stored and the relationships between data items (individuals and groups). The structure of the relationship is often called the 'data architecture'. When logical specification is complete, the planning process moves to the 'physical' data design. This determines how the data will be physically stored. This determines the computer's performance in retrieving and storing data, and hence the costs of using the system.

The transition from logical to physical design uses a technique known as traffic analysis. It involves the following stages:

- Rank applications in terms of frequency of use and complexity
- Analyse storage and retrieval entailed in executing each application
- Summarize the results for the most frequent and the most complex applications, showing the navigation path through the database and the frequency of access to the database along each path.

Traffic analysis provides data designers with early feedback concerning database performance. It may lead the data designer to modify the logical model so as to improve database performance. Before the data design is finalized, it should be checked against the following criteria:

- Minimal storage and I/O activity
- Minimal CPU instructions
- Effective space utilization
- Security
- Flexibility

Implementation

While the detailed design and programming of the database is under way, more detailed design for the physical storage of the data must be developed. As each program is completed, its performance (i.e. productivity) must be tested, as well as whether it works. The database will then need to be 'tuned' as the applications are developed, to ensure that it continues to meet its planned performance targets.

11 Testing and selecting

Successful database marketing requires a strong commitment to testing. The ideal database marketing campaign is one targeted at customers who are likely to respond. We are only likely to achieve the levels of response we need if we identify who is likely to respond, by testing different media to get to customers, different offers to meet their needs, different creative to express our messages to them, and so on. We do not have to go to a market test straight away. We may test campaign planning assumptions by researching our target customers more deeply. We may test certain aspects of our copy or our telemarketing script. But only a market test tells us if our approach actually works.

The value of testing

Every test we undertake is valuable. It allows us to improve the chance of increasing profit and customer satisfaction, by ensuring that every aspect of our campaign is as attuned to customer needs as possible. Testing can reduce the frequency with which we contact customers who are unlikely to be interested in our offer. Testing can help us find the most effective ways of contacting interested customers. Testing also tells us whether a campaign is worth running and, if so, how frequently.

What to test

The aspects to test are:

- Target market – what precisely is the target market? This applies to any aspect of market segmentation, including (in business markets) size and type of business, category of staff within the business, existing products or services used, and (in consumer markets) type and location of housing, income, family structure, age of household members, psychographic or behavioural characteristics.

- Product – are we offering the right product or service to meet the needs of the target market – range, features, colours, etc?
- Pricing – which pricing option is right for the target market?
- Offer – not just the product or service, but how it is packaged to obtain response. This may include elements relating to the value of the product or service e.g. additional services, payment terms, incentives to customers (e.g. discounts, competitions, time of offer close, early response bonus).
- Format/creative – is the presentation of the offer right for the product and target market?
- Contact strategy – are we using the best strategy for the market, product and offer?
- Timing – has the campaign been mounted at the right time? If we aim to replace a product, what is its replacement cycle?
- Frequency – are we contacting customers often enough to sustain the dialogue, but not so frequently as to alienate them?

Test validity

Our conclusions will be valid if we:

- Make sure that the test is run on a large enough sample to ensure that the results are statistically valid.
- Ensure the sample chosen is part of a larger target market with the same characteristics, to which the campaign is to be applied later. Otherwise, this is not a test, but a campaign in its own right.
- Test one variable at a time. If more than one is changed, we cannot be sure which caused any variation in the results.
- Make sure that during testing no market changes affect test results.
- Make sure that the costs for the test campaign bear a clear relationship to the costs for a full campaign, allowing for any savings due to increased volume or artwork costs already incurred.
- Maintain existing promotional efforts to other parts of the target market. We are normally testing on a relative basis – to find whether a campaign is better than one that is currently running. If promotion through sales force incentives was the prime mode of promotion, these incentives should be maintained at least for the period of the test. A control is always required to ensure that the comparison is a true one.

We usually test on the one or all principle. We either test just one campaign variable, by running two or more campaigns, each differing from the other in one respect (e.g. timing), or we test totally different campaigns. If we vary two elements, we cannot be sure which one achieved any improvement in results. We therefore test the most important element of the campaign first.

Many of the above conditions are hard to satisfy in practice. In a fast changing market, it is rarely easy to keep 'other things equal'. Common sense has to be used to check whether changes that have occurred are likely to affect the results of the test. However, in database marketing, an apparently small change (e.g. the positioning of a reply coupon on a page, or the order of questions in a telemarketing script) can produce significant changes in response rates. For this reason, database marketing relies on experiment and testing to improve response rates.

Selecting

Our ability to manage our dialogue with customers depends on our market targeting (identifying the kinds of needs which we can satisfy) and on our ability to select individual customers who have these needs. Successful targeting depends on the information on the database being high quality and on using the right criteria for selecting customers for a campaign.

When we use the database to select customers for a campaign, we need to define a target customer profile. This indicates the kind of customer we want to attract with a particular campaign. We use the computer to match this profile with individual customer profiles. Selection is not easy, but the experimental nature of database marketing and our ability to control our target precisely means we can test the response of a particular list of customers by using only part of it.

The main reasons we make selections from the database are:

- To create the basis for running a test or a full campaign, by extracting data about those customers who form the target market for the campaign
- To create a sample group of customers, whose characteristics we wish to analyse more thoroughly.

We improve campaign effectiveness by prioritizing between customers. We determine priorities and preferred approach routes by using sample data, drawn from tests, to determine what makes customers respond. For a particular campaign aimed at small businesses, we might discover that the customers most likely to respond to a mail shot campaign only after a telephone follow-up are those with a lower number of employees and a history of only responding when prompted by telephone to other campaigns, while those most likely to respond by post without prompting are those with a greater number of employees. When we have found variables which seem to account for customer behaviour, we use these variables to select those customers most likely to respond, and to sort those likely to respond into categories with different recommended contact strategies. As contact strategy costs are high, we use objective analysis as much as possible in arriving at our contact strategies.

The results of testing enable us to expand safely from our sample on a large scale. Below, we provide a brief example of the benefits of so doing. It is important to understand that successful implementation of database marketing relies heavily on this kind of detailed work. Without good testing strategies, the best designed database marketing system has immense potential for laying waste to marketing budgets. We want to know not only which half of advertising works best, but which tenth or even twentieth, and then which is the second best tenth, and so on. Even better, if we find out by testing which are the best customers to focus on before we roll out the campaign to the whole target market, we will minimize waste from the very beginning. We will get the best returns on our marketing communications budgets, while minimizing misdirected communication. This is what the following example demonstrates. It also shows that it may be better to roll out a campaign in two steps. Consider the following results:

Market segment	Total population	First test sample	Results	Second test sample	Results	Full campaign
A1	20 000	1 000	C	1 000	B	10 000
A2	50 000	1 000	A	5 000	A	30 000
B1	10 000	1 000	B	3 000	B	5 000
B2	25 000	1 000	A	5 000	B	10 000
C	100 000	1 000	D	–	–	–

Results key: A = excellent B = good C = marginal D = poor

This table shows that in the first test, we took the same sample sizes from each market segment. We then took a second sample, taking a larger sample from segments which had shown excellent results. Segment B2, which had shown excellent results, shows on a larger sample only good results, not excellent ones. If our objectives and costs indicate the need to target primarily the segments showing excellent response, our campaign numbers might then be as shown in the last column.

Selection: an example

Here is a simplified example of how the combined process of selection and prioritizing might work in a campaign for a new company pensions plan.

Select for initial outbound mailing all service businesses with 20–50 employees with revenue growth in excess of 20 per cent per year. (This would be because businesses not having these characteristics showed significantly lower response and purchase rates in the test campaign.)

The first step in every contact strategy might be to ask the customer to complete a coupon or to telephone us. This is because the test showed that the response rate from customers who were given the choice was higher than from customers who were not given the choice. The returned coupon will be followed up immediately by a telephone call from us. Inbound or outbound calls will use a questionnaire to establish intensity of need/interest.

If the customer responds with coupon or telephone call within two weeks of receiving the promotion, and indicates in the telephone call an urgent need for the product, mail additional information and call for a sales visit. If sales call proves negative, archive the enquiry.

If the customer responds with coupon or telephone call between two and four weeks of receiving the promotion, and indicates in the telephone call an urgent need for the product, mail additional literature and ask customer to confirm by telephone whether a sales call is needed after reading it. If no telephone call is received within two weeks of this, telephone the customer. If no further interest shown, archive the enquiry.

If the customer responds with coupon or telephone call within two weeks of receiving the promotion, and indicates in the telephone call some interest in the product, mail additional information and ask customer to confirm by telephone whether a sales call is needed after reading it. If no call is received within two weeks of this, mail reminder letter. If no further action, archive the enquiry.

If the customer responds with coupon or telephone call between two and four weeks of receiving the promotion, and indicates in the telephone call some interest in the product, mail additional information and ask customer to confirm by telephone whether a sales call is needed after reading it. If no further action, archive the enquiry.

If no response is received, send reminder letter. If still no response, take no further action.

A diagrammatic representation of this contact strategy is shown in Figure 11.1.

Statistical techniques for testing and selection

The use of statistical techniques in increasing sales or reducing costs can best be shown by example. Database marketing relies on the use of sophisticated statistical techniques to convert the power of systems into successful marketing. This requires a level of detailed work which may be unfamiliar to marketers used to big television campaigns.

Our study relates to a direct mail programme to car owners. A million car owners were separated into three groups, as follows:

Group 1   A no-mail control group
Group 2   A group to receive three promotional mailings

Group 3   A group to receive a mailed questionnaire.

The questionnaire covered topics such as the features desired in a car, the qualities associated with the supplier's make, the type of car currently driven, preferred make, mileage, date of delivery, whether privately owned, and expected date of next acquisition. Those who returned the questionnaire completed (Group 3a) were sent three promotional mailings, while those who did not (Group 3b) were not contacted again. Figure 11.2 is an example of the kind of questionnaire used for this purpose. The questionnaire is kept simple to ensure a high response rate.

The test result showed a clear relationship between the contact method and the purchase rate, as follows:

Group	Purchase %
3a	2.5
2	1.95
3b	1.2
1	1.05

The questionnaire data were then used to segment the market and determine the contact strategy for each customer in the subsequent roll-out of the campaign. Statistical tests were used to determine which variables covered in the question-naire were most closely associated with subsequent sales. In this case, 10 out of 50 variables covered by the questionnaire were found to be strongly associ-ated. Not surprisingly, expected timing of next acquisition was closely related to actual purchase. Using these test results, multiple regression techniques were then used to develop a scoring formula shown below. In some cases (e.g. make of current and preferred car) numerical variables had to be created by statistical experimentation. The aim here is to arrive at numerical values which best discriminate between purchasers and non-purchasers of the company's make.

Score =   − 0.02 x Timing (When acquisition intended, in months)
          + 0.001 x Loyalty (Whether last purchase was brand loyal)
          + 0.03 x Age (In years)
          − 0.015 x Preferred make
          + 0.001 x Year of manufacture of current car
          − 0.005 x Make of current car
          − 0.015 x Most preferred next purchase
          − 0.055

Scores were then assigned to each individual based on questionnaire responses. These scores indicated the probability of purchase. Respondents were then ranked according to their score and divided into ten groups (deciles) according to their predicted probability of purchase. This is called a gains chart and is shown in Table 11.1.

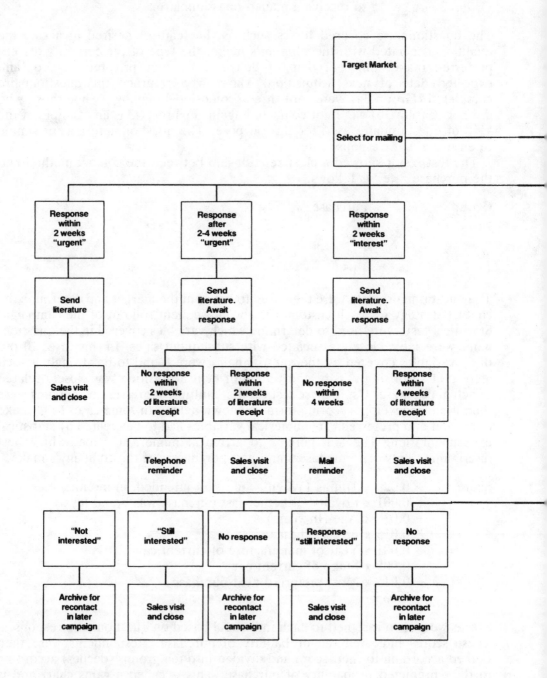

Figure 11.1: Example of a contact strategy

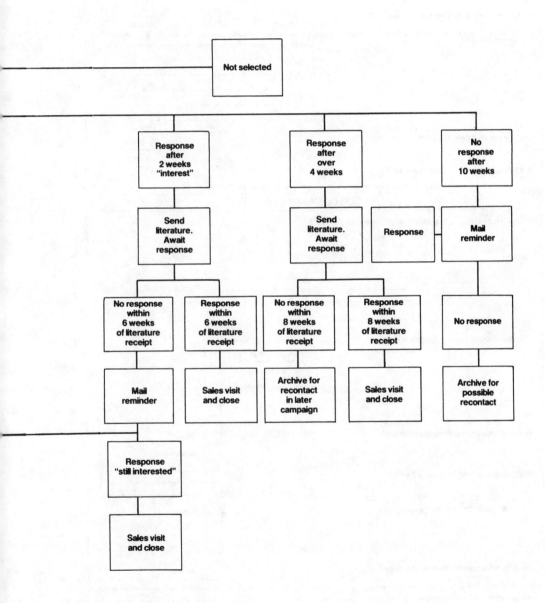

NAME:	TITLE:	SURNAME:		INITIALS:

HOME ADDRESS:

YOUR CAR

How many cars does your household have?

1 ☐   2 ☐   More than 2 ☐

Please answer the following questions about your car. If your household has more than one car, then please answer questions about the second car in the appropriate section (not shown in this illustration).

Make	
Model	
Series	
Engine size	cc
Reg. No.	

Did you obtain it new or used?

New ☐   Used ☐

Is it privately owned or a company car?

Private ☐   Company ☐

If it is a private car, please go straight to the section on your second car and do not answer any more questions in this section.

YOUR COMPANY CAR

Roughly how many cars are there in your company's fleet?

1-5 ☐   6-10 ☐   11-20 ☐   20-50 ☐   51-99 ☐   100+ ☐

Company name:
Your job title:

Can you choose your company car?

Completely free choice ☐

Free choice within price limit
State limit to nearest £000 ☐   Limit:

Free choice from certain makes
State makes ☐   Make:

Choice within price limit and from certain makes
State limit to nearest £000
State makes ☐   Make: Limit:

No choice ☐

When do you expect to replace this car?

☐ Months
☐ No definite time

What do you expect to replace it with?

Make
Model

How frequently do you change your car?

Every ☐ months, or
Every ☐ years, or
Every ☐ 000 miles

Roughly what annual mileage do you do?

☐ 000 miles

Figure 11.2: Customer questionnaire used for scoring and selection

Table 11.1
Gains Chart

Minimum score	%Database (decile)	Cumulative sales%	Gain%
0.090	10	8.0	264
0.060	20	5.5	150
0.050	30	4.5	105
0.040	40	3.9	77
0.035	50	3.5	59
0.033	60	3.2	45
0.028	70	2.9	32
0.026	80	2.6	18
0.022	90	2.4	9
0.020	100	2.2	0

The interpretation of this table is as follows. The first row shows that, based on their responses to the questionnaire, the best 10 per cent of responders would increase the rate of purchase by 264 per cent over that of the entire group of responders. This allows a contact strategy (e.g. mailing frequency) to be established, taking into account mailing economics. An illustration of how contact strategy might be varied is shown in Table 11.2.

Table 11.2
Contact Strategy

Contact	Breakeven sales rate%	%database	Sales Rates
5+ times	5	10	8.0
3 times	3	20	3.0
2 times	2	30	2.4
		40	2.2
1 time	1	50	1.8
		60	1.6
		70	1.2
No follow-up		80	0.8
		90	0.5
		100	0.2

This illustrates some important general rules:

1. The impact of database marketing programmes is often determined mainly by the number and timing of contacts. In particular
   - The best customers and prospects will support more contacts
   - When a purchasing decision is infrequent and planned, as with automobiles, contact planning becomes more important

- Response is highest when products most important to the respondent are presented first and the offers repeated often.
2. Statistical models aid in determining contact strategy by:
   - Ranking customers and prospects to identify those who merit more or fewer contacts
   - Identifying some elements to which each prospect is most likely to respond, thereby helping set the best sequence of contacts
3. The database marketing system must manage the data to assure the generation of the desired contact at the appointed time.

Many statistical approaches can be used in database marketing. They differ in their relevance, ease of use, data requirements etc. Statistical techniques are essential, but failure will result from assigning an inexperienced statistician, perhaps a university graduate in statistics or econometrics, to the problems of database marketing. Database marketing requires a high level of attention to detail. Because of the measurability of database marketing, we have the data on which to deploy statistical techniques to replace the intuition that characterized so much marketing policy making in the past. But these techniques must be used correctly.

Some examples of the kinds of technique used may bring this point home. The examples we have chosen are:

- Multiple regression
- Cell population analysis
- Cluster analysis

Multiple regression

Multiple regression is a classic technique for describing the relationship between a target variable and other variables. It is usually summarized in the form of an equation 'explaining' the target variable in terms of other variables. It is widely used and can be used to analyse both quantitative and qualitative variables. However, it may require more computer resource and analyst time than other techniques. Its main strength is its ability to draw conclusions from a relatively small number of observations. A corresponding disadvantage is that it requires considerable skill to use it properly. Models derived using this technique are fairly difficult to apply in practice.

Cell analysis

Cell analysis involves grouping sample members into different cells, each defined by combining two or more variables by which members are measured. For example, FRAC analysis (Frequency, Recency, Amount and Category) can be used to group sample members according to the frequency with which they have purchased, the date of last purchase, the amount and type of purchase. The cells are then tested for differences between each other using various techniques. An example of cell analysis is shown in Table 11.3.

Table 11.3
Cell analysis – example

| Recency of last purchase | Revenue per thousand customers | | | | |
| | Number of prior purchases | | | | |
	1	2 – 3	4 – 5	6+	All
0 – 3 months	2302	4019	6213	9850	3521
4 – 6 months	1721	2900	4820	7473	2602
7 – 12 months	1188	2288	2921	3995	1920
13 – 24 months	991	1840	2680	3400	1470
All	1525	2620	3997	4682	2313

This table shows that, for example, customers who are in the top left hand cell (i.e who have made only one prior purchase, and that purchase was in the last three months) had an average spend of £2302, compared with the average of £1525 for those who had only made one purchase, and £3521 for all those who bought in the last three months. The averages are of course weighted for the number of customers in each cell (not shown). We might, depending on the cost of accessing these customers and results of other analyses, decide that only customers in certain cells were worth targeting for our next campaign.

For this analysis to be statistically valid, there must be enough members in each cell, so it can require quite large sample sizes. This implies that a sample population should not be broken down into too many cells by the use of too many variables to describe the population. The advantages of this technique is that it requires limited skill and that the appropriate computer software is widely available. The skill is required more in finding (or constructing) variables which are used to define the cells. But once models are obtained using these techniques, they are amongst the easiest to implement. They are also amongst the easiest to understand intuitively, if presented correctly. The results are presentable in simple tabular form. This makes it easier for top management to get to grips with what can seem to be a rather tortuous statistical process.

Cluster and discriminant analysis

Cluster and discriminant analysis groups members of a population by their overall similarity on specified characteristics. Discriminant analysis is used to find characteristics that best discriminate between different groups. These approaches are intuitively quite appealing – we tend to want to group (or segment) customers into categories with different characteristics. Indeed, much recent progress in market segmentation analysis has used these techniques.

However, this is usually only one of the first steps in an analysis. One or other of the above mentioned approaches then needs to be used to analyse response rates and sales of the different groups of customers.

Computer software for applying these techniques is less widely available. It requires fairly advanced statistical knowledge to apply and interpret their results. Computer resource requirements are also higher. Further, models resulting from these analyses can be difficult to apply in practice.

Preparation for testing

If we do not do our selection homework, we may test many lists and media and never get good results. We must find out as much as possible about the list or the medium's coverage and the behaviour of the people it covers, such as:

- Are the names and addresses accurate and not duplicated?
- How recently have the list and the relevant data on it been used?
- How recently have the people on the list responded to promotion?
- How often have they received a promotion?
- How often do they respond?
- How quickly do they respond?
- How seriously do they respond i.e. with intent to purchase?
- How often do they buy a product of the kind being sold?
- Do they buy directly from particular media?
- What is their likely average order value?
- How do they prefer to pay – cash, credit card, etc.?
- How quickly do they pay?
- Who uses the list successfully?
- Can we select the target customer we want?

If we are using an outside list, additional questions are:

- What selections are possible, and at what cost?
- What is the minimum selection size for a test?
- What addressing formats are available (e.g. label, tape)?
- Is the list postcoded?
- Is it coded with any other standard classification (e.g. PINPOINT, SIC)?

The answers to these questions are needed in making campaign selections. Their answers, together with information on the target market for the campaign, give us the criteria for selecting our test lists. The tests will also tell us how often we can use the list without wearout of response.

Making testing comprehensive

A comprehensive testing programme must:

- Test the main campaign elements all the time (offer, media/list, creative, target market) and not fine tune while these elements are untested
- Test frequency and timing of campaigns – more difficult because external factors change over time and may affect test results
- Analyse the results, which should then be acted upon
- Test large enough samples for the results to be valid. The validity of the test depends upon the sample size, not that of the planned final campaign
- Test representative samples
- Test only one variable at a time
- Ensure that test costs bear a clear relationship to full campaign costs, to allow accurate extrapolation
- Use a control group.

Many of these conditions are hard to satisfy in practice. Other things never remain equal. So a degree of common sense is required is making assumptions about what variables are likely to influence test results. But care must be taken here, as results are often affected by variables which are apparently unimportant.

Forecasting

The accuracy of the test-based forecast for the roll-out of the main campaign depends on:

- The representativeness of the test.
- Changes to the product, offer and creative.
- List quality.
- Time of year or month.

The variability of forecasts leads most database marketers to be conservative in their forecasts, particularly in new markets, or where radically different marketing policies are being tried. But as experience with a market and product grows, forecasting becomes more precise and confident.

12   The marketing workbench

'It is now technically possible to wire up the nation so that a corporate marketing executive can get instant reports on sales as they happen. And that leads to a fantasy view of the future brand manager, sitting like Captain Kirk on the bridge of the Starship Enterprise, getting reports on sales and then directing the specialists in his marketing crew to pour on instant consumer incentives where competition demands.' *New York Times*, 20 June 1984.

Some elements of this vision can be achieved today. This chapter discusses technology that can be installed today to support the current activities of marketing managers.

The marketing workbench, the electronic office, office automation – all these are terms for a technological revolution which is already making its mark and will change the way marketers work over the next decade. Most marketing departments are using some of this technology. Personal computers are being used to model brand behaviour, using spreadsheets and more advanced packages. Word processors, telex and facsimile machines are now standard business equipment and often used to communicate with customers. Much of this machinery is presently bought and used independently. The key to the future lies in the convergence and integration of these facilities and technologies, so that information recorded at several locations and in a variety of forms can readily be stored and accessed regardless of where it was created and in what medium.

Where is the technology today?

The term 'marketing workbench' broadly describes the application of electronic aids to the functions of a marketing office. At present, these aids take a variety of forms, such as;

- Relational databases, which support the indexing and rapid retrieval of management information held in an electronic form. Such databases are referred to as marketing management information systems (MMIS).
- End user and personal computing facilities, which make information directly available for examination and manipulation by decision makers and professional staff. This information might be extracted from the MMIS, obtained from a third party who makes it available on a commercial basis, or might be created directly by the user.
- Electronic publishing facilities, which are used to type, edit and prepare documents combining text, data and graphics.
- Electronic mail systems, which allow documents and messages to be transferred quickly and easily between individuals who may be in the same location of a company, or in different companies.
- Voice systems which can record and send voice messages, resembling a combination of telephone answering and electronic mail systems.

The impact of technology

The effect of increased technology will be to make marketing management more effective in all their managerial activities. It will increase the availability of information to support decision making. Perhaps the best way of describing the impact of the workbench is through examples.

Example 1

1. A middle manager in the advertising department receives a call from a customer who is complaining about the non-delivery of literature that he has requested. The manager takes the call on his marketing workbench – consisting of combination of a personal computer and a telephone. As the customer is talking, the manager enters the customer's name into his computer and retrieves the customer's file. He reads it and sees the literature request and also notes on the file the history of poor service to this particular customer.
2. Still using the workbench, the manager checks the status of literature fulfilment and discovers that the literature has been sent out that day, and reassures the customer.
3. After the customer has rung off, the manager keys in a command to send

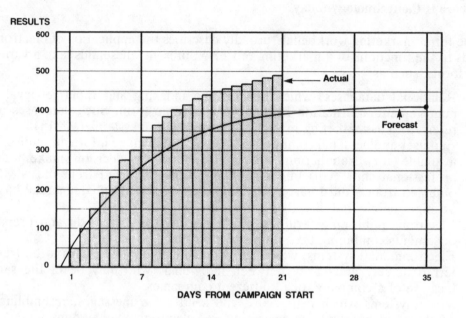

Figure 12.1: Campaign response curves – actual and forecast

a letter of apology with a gift to the customer, and to track delivery performance for that customer's next five orders and enquiries.
4. The manager then types a brief memo to literature fulfilment and sends it through the electronic mail system, with copies to the manager responsible for all fulfilment operations.
5. Finally, the manager reviews the overall percentage of late deliveries by the fulfilment operation. Finding that there is an increasing problem, he uses his workbench to plot figures over the last 12 months (see Figure 12.1). These show responses running ahead of forecast, indicating that the problem was possibly due to a literature shortage. He forwards the graph with a covering letter to the literature department.

Example 2

1. The marketing manager receives a request via electronic mail from a product manager for the running of a tactical direct marketing campaign to boost the returns from a campaign which is in the field but is showing slightly lower performance than forecast. This is causing a surplus of inventory.
2. The marketing manager uses his terminal to check the current inventory situation and the latest campaign results to confirm whether the situation is serious enough to warrant the additional expenditure. He also checks

whether marketing expenditure to date allows him the leeway to spend the money, taking into account planned expenditures and contingencies.

3. He examines campaign performance to identify whether the problem has been due to poor initial response, poor conversion rates or any other factor. When he has identified the reasons for the poor performance, he uses the library of previously used contact strategies for similar campaigns to identify whether any other contact strategy would be better than the one used, given what has been learnt from the current campaign so far. If more than one contact strategy has been used for the current campaign, he also verifies which contact strategy has been most productive for the current campaign, and works out what would be the consequences of using it for the tactical campaign.

4. Using the results to date, he checks what expenditure would be required to bring responses up to target level, and calculates what impact the expenditure would have on the product budget.

5. He checks the state of stocks of the relevant literature, telemarketing capacity etc., to see whether the proposed contact strategy for the tactical campaign is feasible, given resources.

6. If it is, he uses electronic mail to confirm that a tactical campaign is feasible, indicating the likely costs and results and asking for the product manager's approval to brief an agency.

All this could be implemented using currently available technology. A possible configuration for such a system is shown in Figure 12.2.

A marketing workbench should greatly improve the breadth, depth and quality of the information available to management. But this improvement will not happen automatically. Technology provides the physical means of storing, delivering and manipulating the information, but cannot guarantee its quality, depth and relevance. Understanding the information needs of management and developing the systems procedures required to provide it is the first step in developing such a system.

Many companies are developing marketing systems of some kind. Many of these systems are single problem oriented. Few address broad strategic needs. Without a company-wide strategy there is a danger of different groups developing different approaches and acquiring incompatible equipment. Developing the strategy involves the following steps:

1. Determine the areas of highest potential for the use of technology in the marketing office and in the field, and analyse needs in detail.

2. Assess the current status of data processing and office automation in the marketing office and analyse the use to which it is being put.

3. Assess the impact of the company's business plan on the need for a marketing workbench.

4. Develop a marketing workbench strategy which addresses:

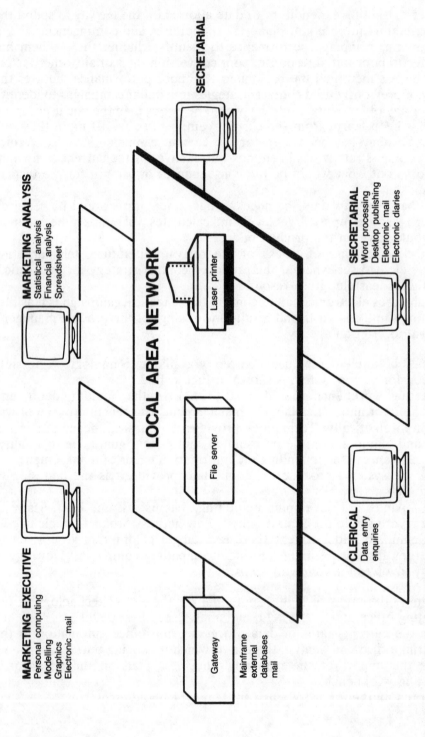

MARKETING EXECUTIVE
Personal computing
Modelling
Graphics
Electronic mail

MARKETING ANALYSIS
Statistical analysis
Financial analysis
Spreadsheet

SECRETARIAL

LOCAL AREA NETWORK

Laser printer

File server

Gateway
Mainframe
external
databases
mail

SECRETARIAL
Word processing
Desktop publishing
Electronic mail
Electronic diaries

CLERICAL
Data entry
enquiries

Figure 12.2: Marketing workbench network configuration

- The desired status of the marketing department's facilities in 3–5 years' time
- The need for integration of data processing and office automation technologies and the practicalities of integration
- The steps necessary to move from the current position to the position in 3–5 years' time, including the desirability or otherwise of pilot testing new facilities before embarking on large scale investment.

Integrating marketing systems

In many companies, marketing systems are a long way from delivering the workbench. There may be several marketing and sales systems, none of which are capable of working with each other. They may need to be accessed through different terminals. They are likely to require very different skill levels to operate them. They may be the subject of intense organizational politics, in the sense that different systems are owned by different departments, who may be unwilling to sacrifice total control to enable the whole company to obtain the benefits of integration.

The only remedy for this situation in a company which develops its systems by consensus is to work hard, possibly over several years, to develop a consensus about what is needed, and influence the consensus in the right direction by developing prototype systems which deliver benefits to all parties. In a company where systems decisions are taken in a more directive manner from the top, the chief executive may be the person who needs to be persuaded of the value of such an integrated marketing system.

Success factors

The marketing workbench will not work without the right information. The information to manage a database marketing organization is needed to ensure:

1. *Quantifiability*. The results (costs and benefits) of every marketing action should be quantified in detail.
2. *Ability to test, research and experiment*. This derives from the quantifiability of the information, but also from the fact that database marketing requires complete control over what is tested and the manner in which it is tested. Experimental activity is performed, as far as possible, under rigidly controlled conditions. This is to ensure that the factor being tested is the only one that varies. In practice, database marketers do not benefit from a laboratory environment. Further, the normal marketing environment is not that of the physical scientist. If database marketing is to achieve high standards of testing, management attention must focus on controlling

testing, research and experimentation in the market place. The secret of success is to build the necessary scientific controls into the normal marketing management process.

3. *Capability of being disruptive, harmful and dangerous.* Millions of letters can be sent to the wrong people. Hundreds of leads can be sent to the sales force, before the latter have been briefed on the campaign. Dozens of tests can be run when there is no mechanism to record the data required to analyse tests. Although the basic management disciplines of database marketing are not new, management must be more forceful in applying them if database marketing is to succeed for the company as a whole. Three factors must be watched particularly carefully:

- Customer management, including analysis of customers acquired and lost, contact strategies used for them, and their lifetime value
- Financial management, in terms of the profitability of every test and campaign
- Timing management, or controlling the management process.

These are dealt with in the following chapters.

13 Customer management

Customers are expensive to acquire and not easy to keep. A company that neglects the acquisition and retention of customers will incur high marketing costs relative to any competitors that take more trouble. The marketing workbench must therefore give an accurate and up to date picture of acquisition and retention. The relevant management report is the customer inventory. This shows customer gains and losses, classified in various ways (e.g. by type of customer, type of product typically bought). Figure 13.1 shows an example of such an inventory.

Table 13.1
Customer inventory

Segment	Prior year end	Added to database	Purged from database	Current count	Net change
Male A	5 500 000	600 000	200 000	5 900 000	400 000
Male B	2 350 000	150 000	50 000	2 450 000	100 000
Male C	1 230 000	80 000	200 000	1 110 000	−120 000
Female D	8 490 000	970 000	270 000	9 190 000	700 000
Female E	4 360 000	330 000	730 000	3 960 000	−400 000
Female F	2 030 000	150 000	120 000	2 060 000	30 000

The concept of customer lifetime value

If acquiring customers is expensive, why do it? Over the period of a customer's relationship with us, he may buy many times, across all our product range. To take this into account, we use the notion of the lifetime value of the customer. This measures the net present value of all future contributions to overhead and profit from the customer. To estimate the lifetime value of a group of customers acquired through a particular marketing action, we need data on:

- All our marketing contacts with the customer
- The responses and revenues that result from these contacts
- The costs associated with each action and response
- Change in status of customers, e.g. between being a customer and not being one, or from being an intense user to an infrequent user
- The present value of future profits.

The concept of lifetime value can cause a company to reassess the way it does business. Many companies overlook ways of creating a continuing and growing stream of profitable income. Examples of long term revenue streams that can be created include:

- Warranty and service revenues on equipment and installations
- Pension, investment and insurance schemes
- Club subscriptions

Policies which increase the revenue stream from a given set of customers increase the lifetime value of these customers. We use the concept of lifetime value when we have to answer questions such as:

- How much should we pay to recruit new customers?
- What is it worth to us to reactivate lapsed customers?
- Which customers are profitable to us, and how profitable are they?

If we take the concept of lifetime value of customers to its logical conclusion, our customers become a marketing asset in the full sense of the term. We should already view them as an asset, as part of our fundamental marketing creed. But they become a solid financial asset when we have identified the profit streams which arise from them. The profit stream is of course the revenue stream less the costs of obtaining it. In accounting terms, this is good will. Each customer is valued by the present value of his profit stream. We can then analyse our market to establish which segments are growing in present value and which shrinking.

Let us examine how the concept of lifetime value is applied. Take the example of an office equipment company, selling items of equipment which require servicing and which use consumables such as stationery, diskettes, printer ribbons and the like. As shown in Figure 13.1, the initial sale of the product

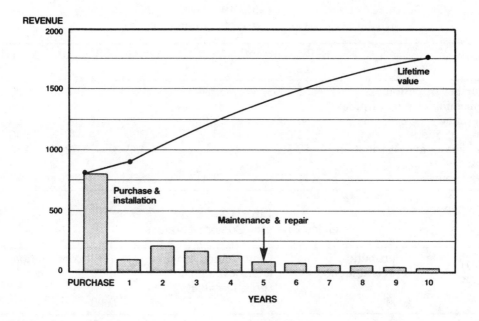

Figure 13.1: Product and service revenue streams

may bring immediate 'after-market' revenue in the form of installation charges and an extended warranty contract. Once the initial sale is completed, there is a continuing stream after the warranty has expired. Further revenue comes from replacements, changes, upgrades, additional software, supplies, support and service contracts, post-sale consultancy and the like. The equipment sale may be preceded by consultancy services. Although such services, like the installation charges and initial guarantee costs, may be 'bundled' into the initial price, they nonetheless constitute separate revenues.

On this calculation, with service and warranty charges usually around 10–15 per cent of equipment price, and installation costs up to 30 per cent of the equipment price for very complex equipment, total revenue from the product may exceed that for the initial item of equipment by a multiple of 2 or 3, even assuming no upgrade or sale of additional products. If we include these items, the multiple may be 10 or more. Given the high lifetime value relative to initial sale revenue, customer acquisition should be treated as an investment. In our example, the revenue/cost profile of a group of customers might be as depicted in Table 13.2.

Here, the future profit stream pays for the initial investment in obtaining the customer. In many industries, the revenue streams from customers are predictable enough to allow rules of thumb to be used in fixing investment in customer acquisition.

Table 13.2
Customer profit stream

Year	Recruitment year	Year 1	Year 2	Year 3	Year 4
Number of customers remaining at start of period	1 000	980	960	940	920
Revenue	80 000	22 000	18 400	10 800	6 800
Cost of goods	32 000	8 800	7 360	4 640	3 040
Marketing and distribution costs	59 332	4 788	4 452	3 272	2 716
Contribution	(11 332)	8 412	6 588	2 888	1 044

Table 13.3
Gains Chart for Customer Values

Decile	Contribution on recruitment £000	Contribution from later development (present value) £000	Total contribution £000
1	445	1214	1659
2	290	890	1180
3	172	607	779
4	112	487	599
5	59	300	359
6	25	290	315
7	0	257	257
8	(17)	214	197
9	(35)	172	137
10	(56)	43	(13)

A company using the lifetime value approach would contact *more* customers than if they did not use this approach. Table 13.3 shows how this might look when presented in the form of a gains chart. In this case, the short term orientation would imply contacting customers down to decile 6 or 7, while the longer term orientation would imply also contacting deciles 8 and 9 as well.

In the case of our office equipment company, let us consider how a new product introduction might be handled. Suppose that product A had the following characteristics:

Life cycle   Introduced 10 years ago, now a mature product. Average customer keeps for 7 years.

Customers: New customers still being acquired. Old customers switching to competition due to high perceived cost of service.

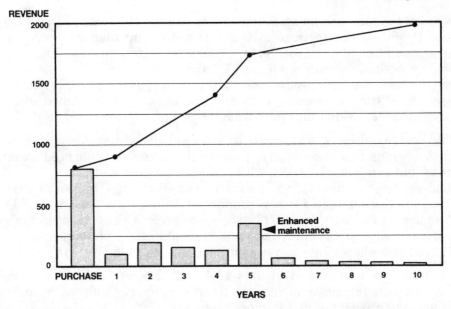

Figure 13.2: Revenue stream from product A: Enhanced maintenance

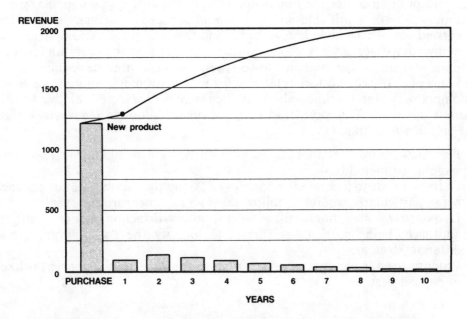

Figure 13.3: Revenue stream from product B: Fault tolerant computer

Two new products are being introduced to combat the switching problem – product B with lower service costs and enhanced maintenance product A, involving a substantial overhaul and lower subsequent service costs. The revenue streams for both are shown in Figure 13.2 and 13.3.

The problem is: which customers should be targeted for which product? An analysis of existing customers provides the answer. This shows that our customers can be divided into four separate groups:

1. Old small customers, who prefer to service their existing equipment rather than upgrade or replace it. They are likely targets for enhanced maintenance, but care must be taken when the product is at mid-age.
2. Mid-age large customers, who prefer to upgrade to a new improved product. They are likely targets for new product B.
3. Mid-age smaller customers. They should be given a clear choice in the sales process, using qualification questions to identify their preference.
4. Recent customers. They are primarily targets for enhanced maintenance.

This information is shown in Figures 13.4 and 13.5. Armed with this information, we can target campaigns at these customers, with each customer receiving an approach tailored to meet his needs.

Getting the concept accepted

The concept of customer life time value is well established in companies whose customers are all identifiable and with whom successive financial transactions are carried out. These include mail order and financial services companies. But for many companies, this is a new concept, or one that is poorly understood. In some companies, the pressure to sell 'new business' militates against use of the concept. This can distort relationships with customers, and even alienate customers with high lifetime values, as they may be neglected relative to their business potential. This problem can be resolved, although it may take time. One solution is as follows:

• First make sure that lifetime value statistics are available, at least on a sample, estimated basis.
• Carry out tests to indicate the benefits of taking the lifetime value approach, being particularly careful to follow through and measure the results.
• Demonstrate the financial and customer-satisfaction benefits of the approach, being particularly careful to identify the cut-off points under different strategies.
• Propose specific changes to policy in areas where using the concept is likely to pay off best.

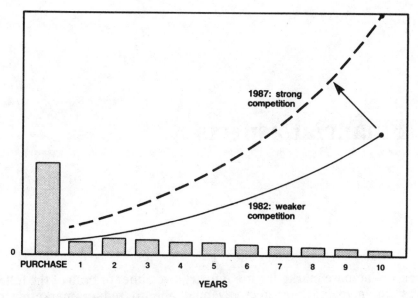

Figure 13.4: Rate of switching to competitors

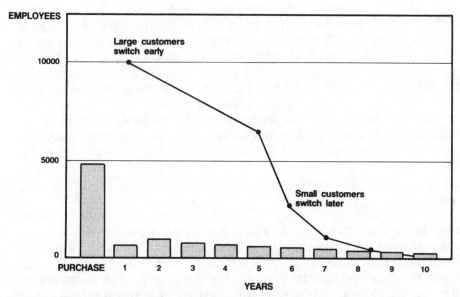

Figure 13.5: Average size of customers who are switching

14   Financial aspects

Most users of database marketing use it to achieve either or both of the following objectives: to increase or protect revenue; and to reduce marketing costs. Although immediate objectives may be framed in other terms (e.g. customer recruitment), final objectives are usually those stated above. However, some users of database marketing techniques are non-profit organizations. While some (such as charities) do use database marketing to generate revenue or reduce costs, others use it for different reasons. For example, trade unions use it to create a stronger dialogue with their members. Political parties use it to recruit and stay in touch with members. Government departments may use it to ensure that citizens exercise their rights. Such organizations may also thereby increase revenue and reduce administrative costs, but these are not the primary objectives. For them, the value which is the 'output' of database marketing is measured not by increased revenue, reduced costs and profit but by other variables. Although throughout this book we use the language of profitability and revenue, this does not diminish its relevance to organizations which measure value and costs in other ways.

Back to basics

In analysing the revenue effects of database marketing, we start with the very fundamentals of marketing. A company is considered as a 'brand' – in the full sense of the term. That is to say, a (brand) image of the company is present in actual and potential customers' minds. This image gives the company an 'opportunity' to develop a relationship with customers, expressed through a dialogue. In this dialogue, products are sold, information and money are transferred, and the brand image is fortified. The dialogue is carried out through various media and channels, and relates to a variety of products. If a company operates in many markets with many types of customer, there may be many such brands – but the fundamental argument is the same.

It can be argued that in the long run, the only marketing asset a company has is its brand image in customers' minds. The rest – products, distribution channels, marketing communications – are merely ways through which the relationship with customers is reinforced and by which revenue and profit are obtained during the dialogue. Of course, we cannot ignore the presence of factories turning out products, of inventories of finished goods, of retail stores waiting for customers to visit them, and of well trained sales staff with good customer and product knowledge. But without their ability to attract customers and give value to them, they are worth nothing in marketing terms.

This view of marketing is a little frightening – it lacks the 'stakes in the ground' which characterize the more conventional view of business, in which existing products, production resources and real estate are seen as the chief assets. However, there are three reasons why this 'back to basics' view of marketing is important:

1. *Rising importance of service industries.* The proportion of GNP that is accounted for by manufactured products is still falling and is well below half the GNP in developed economies. Customers needs are increasingly met through services. Although service products require some degree of 'hard' commitment (e.g. retail sites, information systems), they may still be much more alterable to meet customer needs than many manufactured products. This flexibility is increasing, as service companies get sharper at changing their products to meet these needs. This has led advanced service company practitioners of database marketing, such as motoring associations, publishing companies, and financial services suppliers, to spread their activities into a variety of other fields, exploiting their chief marketing assets (brand name and customer base).

2. *Greater service component of 'hard' products.* The service component is increasing. This can be measured crudely by the difference between the manufacturing cost and the final price. In consumer markets, as income and wealth increase, consumers are happier to pay higher prices for 'value-added' products, where the value is added not principally by enhanced physical formulation, but by advertising, availability in the 'right' outlet, and sales and after-sales service. In industrial markets, many buyers have realized the importance of buying not on price but on value for money. Value includes all the service elements of the product. If price is the sole criterion, the customer may end up incurring high costs after the purchase.

3. *'Myopia' induced by existing sales channels.* Many suppliers' view of their marketing position is constrained by their existing sales channels. They may rely

on their existing sales channels to create their branding, perhaps by packaging or point of sale material for retail display, or by training their sales force to present the branding appropriately. Or their method of creating branding may be tied to the particular channels they use. For example they may use heavy television advertising to create 'pull' for their product in retail stores. However, database marketing often opens up new channel possibilities, in which the sole initial marketing assets are brand image and customer base.

How does all this relate to revenue stream analysis? Revenue stream analysis identifies actual and potential revenue streams flowing from customer to company. It then analyses how applying the principles of database marketing can lead to realization of potential revenue streams and more effective management of existing ones – irrespective of current products and sales channels. Although these physical components of the marketing mix may impose constraints on revenue stream analysis, in many cases they do not. To make the most of database marketing, we must be particularly careful to avoid the myopia that constrains us to existing products, channels and modes of promotion.

Improving branding and the revenue stream

Let us look at an example of how a company can use database marketing techniques to improve or extend its branding, increase revenue or cut costs. Take the case of a manufacturer of vending equipment, currently selling through its own direct sales force and through distributors. We assume a starting position in which sales staff and distributors have their own prospect and customer files. However, they have no structured programme for enhancing their quality, for maintaining dialogue with customers and prospects according to their propensity to purchase, and no procedure for directly tying marketing objectives and strategies to the needs of customers as expressed through their relationship with the company. Instead, market research is used to provide sample data.

Database marketing helps such a company develop its revenue streams and reduce its costs in a number of ways, as follows:

● Providing improved mechanisms for handling unstimulated demand. For example, information about customers telephoning in to enquire about the availability of particular products or features may be lost. Providing a mechanism for this information to be received in a structured way, by setting up an inbound telemarketing facility, may not only increase sales of existing products, but provide direction for new product development, both within its existing product area and in new areas. The information from this facility may indicate that the company's brand image extends well beyond its existing product line (e.g. up- or down-market, into other product areas or services).

- Developing new leads for existing equipment for its sales force and distributors, thereby widening the market for its products and ensuring that competitors do not get there first. For example, a combined direct mail and telemarketing operation, working initially on purchased lists, may be used to provide leads from businesses not covered by existing channels (perhaps because of their infrequent purchasing or their location).

- Ensuring effective qualification of prospects, reducing sales force costs and allowing effort to be focused on the best prospects. For example, the telemarketing operation could take over the prospect files of sales staff, and initiate a more structured dialogue with customers. This would indicate when they were in the market.

- Providing customers with a way to express which channel or channels (direct sales force, distributor or direct order) they prefer to do business through. For example, a combined trade press and mailing campaign, giving customers alternative initial routes of contact, and a short questionnaire administered in the early stages of the dialogue, would allow the customer to indicate clearly the preferred contact route and also to receive advice on the best source of supply.

- Developing and defending the market for supplies by providing easier and more cost-effective ways of reordering. For example, a regularly mailed catalogue, with incentives for structured ordering combined with credit facilities and rapid delivery, would encourage customers to plan their supplies ordering effectively.

- Providing a way of ordering machines direct. For example, some customers may not want a salesperson to call, but may prefer a simple reorder. However, they may have found it difficult to obtain information about new models and about the ordering process. This could be handled through regular catalogue distribution, together with an inbound telemarketing operation for provision of more information and for order taking.

- Providing more effective support to distributors, who may have found it difficult to get information from the company, sales leads, supplies and parts. All these can be handled by a telemarketing operation.

- Providing more accurate data for new product design. An outbound mailing and telemarketing operation, working initially from sales staff's files, from customer records, and perhaps purchased lists, but eventually from the customer database, can be used to survey customers and prospects directly, and eventually provide leads for resulting new product sales.

- Ensuring that new products are launched in the right target markets and that existing products are targeted correctly, using a similar process to the above.

- Providing better customer care. A telemarketing operation could be used to deal with customer queries (inbound) and to engage in proactive (outbound) work to establish whether customers are satisfied. This can have a very powerful effect on reinforcing positive branding.

- Identifying prospects for maintenance and service sales. Working on past sales records, a telemarketing operation could be used to identify prospects and to close the sale.
- Identifying markets for related products (i.e. those which its branding would allow the company to supply cost-effectively), such as catering and industrial hygiene. A combined telemarketing and mail operation could be used to survey customer needs and attitudes.

Budgeting and managing campaign costs

The financial opportunities in using database marketing are large. But how do we make sure we capture them? The immense amount of detailed work required to establish a database marketing system and to mount database marketing campaigns implies a very detailed approach to budgeting. For campaign costs, the budget should be built from a zero base, for every year and for every campaign.

The steps required to build a budget for an individual campaign (in this case, a campaign for achieving sales) are as follows:

1. Specify the end result required by the campaign. This should be in terms of sales and profit, and be based on testing.
2. Calculate the number of leads or enquiries required to achieve this sales level. This should be based on a forecast of the lead to sale conversion ratio, and also on tests.
3. Calculate the expected response to the mail shot, coupon, telemarketing outbound call, etc. Testing should also be used to establish this, though in some cases results from similar campaigns in similar media are used to provide an estimate.
4. Work out the response rate to any follow-up activity (e.g. a second letter or telephone call).
5. Calculate the total outbound activity required to achieve the desired response (e.g. initial mailing volume).
6. Work out the average costs and total costs for achieving this (mail, telephone, sales force, etc.)
7. Calculate expected total revenues and contribution and thence expected total profit.
8. Check for consistency with budgeted profit and for superiority over alternative means of achieving the same sales results.
9. If favourable, put campaign into budget and proceed with campaign planning.

In drawing up the budget, we must identify all the activities required to complete the campaign. Ideally, we should be working from a standard project task list, which is connected to a standard cost list.

For example, for a mail order campaign, the budget needs to include promotional costs, such as origination and artwork changes, print and production, list rental, computer analysis, addressing, inserting and postage. It must also include product costs, such as product manufacture and packaging, fulfilment, handling, returns handling, postage, refurbishing, and debt servicing. The budget should only be finalized after testing. For example, in mail order we might want to test deluxe and simple products and packaging.

Campaign effectiveness

There are many criteria by which we can judge a campaign. In the end, the most important results are customer satisfaction and brand support, and how these are translated into financial measures, such as revenue and profit. We can use intermediate criteria to judge effectiveness. These are based on the chain of productivity, the succession of ratios which determine the relationship between input and output. A simple example of such a chain is:

Profit	= Unit profit	x	Number of units sold
Number of units sold	= Sales per lead	x	Number of leads
Number of Leads	= Leads per customer reached	x	Number of customers reached

Using intermediate measures, the campaign could be evaluated by:

- The number of customers it reaches
- How many leads it generates
- Number of demonstrations made
- Number of sales appointments made
- Number of returns
- How many sales it generates
- Incremental profit from the campaign
- How much it increases customer lifetime value.

Each campaign must be evaluated against other types of campaign as well as in conjunction with them (e.g. mail parallel to telemarketing, covering different customers, and mail *vs.* telemarketing, covering all customers, and of course, mail with telemarketing as a combined contact strategy).

We also use 'cost productivity' statistics to judge the effectiveness of different inputs into the marketing process. These include:

- Cost per 1000 mailed or per phone call
- Cost per decision maker contact
- Cost per lead achieved
- Cost per order.

These should be compared for different media and channels, and against the cost of doing business by existing means.

Key performance indicators (KPIs)

The ratios we have just discussed are classic direct marketing ratios, born from years of experience of direct marketing campaigns. The database marketing approach requires a more comprehensive treatment of performance ratios. We need to examine financial performance of all ways of creating and sustaining a relationship with the customer. The indicators we use must therefore be applicable to all channels, which from a database marketing point of view are treated alike, as competitors for marketing resources. Let us start this analysis by considering how KPIs should be used.

The main purpose of having KPIs is to help:

- Sales staff (whether in the field or in branches or retail outlets) to adjust their tactics to improve day to day effectiveness (productivity, profitability, quality, etc.). Thus, a telemarketing team might receive reports showing the productivity of contact strategies for a particular type of customer and product, and revise these strategies. Or a salesperson might receive a report showing the productivity of his/her calling pattern, and revise the pattern.
- Sales management (e.g. sales, telemarketing) to assess the relative effectiveness of marketing mix policies designed to achieve given strategies. Thus, regional marketing management might receive a report showing that in their region telemarketing was more than usually effective in marketing a particular product to a particular kind of customer, and switch resources into telemarketing.
- Head office marketing management to assess whether sales staff are implementing particular strategies with appropriate effectiveness. Thus, a product marketing manager might receive a report showing significant regional variations in sales productivity for his product, and decide to investigate the reasons for this. Or a sector marketing manager might receive a report showing that, over all channels, his set of customers was not being contacted frequently and effectively enough for his revenue targets to be met.
- Head office marketing management to choose between strategies. Thus, they might receive a report showing that in certain customer groups and for certain products, the sales force working together with telemarketing was a more effective marketing combination than any other channel. Or it might receive a report indicating that a particular product was being cross-sold very frequently amongst customers who had not been included in the target for the product, indicating a need to revise market targeting.
- Head office marketing management to assess the overall effectiveness of different parts of the marketing operation and the operation as a whole.

Thus, they might receive a report indicating that return on investment in telemarketing was rising, while the return to retailing was falling.
- General management to assess the effectiveness of the marketing operation as a whole. They might receive a report relating marketing costs to revenues, overall and for particular products and customer groups.

These different applications of KPIs would be based on the same types of report, but typically the further down the list, the greater the level of aggregation (across products, customers and regions).

Problems with KPIs

Many companies have experimented with comprehensive sales and marketing reporting systems, only to discover that their contribution to improving effectiveness can be limited or even negative. The main reasons for this include:

- The time taken to collect and input the data (typically by sales, telemarketing or counter staff) is not justified by the improvement in management information and consequent improvements in policy. In some cases, the time required to collect the data may reduce the productivity of field marketing staff, by turning them into researchers.
- The motivation to input the data honestly and/or accurately is absent. The data are either not entered at all, invented or deliberately falsified. The latter is particularly likely if the data are seen to be a way to keep a check on field marketing staff.
- Too many reports are produced, and too little resource devoted to developing ways to make them comprehensible and actionable. Management is unable to see the wood for the trees.
- The data required are perceived by the staff providing them to dig too deep into factors which are considered to relate to 'personal effectiveness', e.g. personal time and project management, which are considered to be an issue between a member of staff and his line manager, and not for public consumption. The member of staff may therefore enter what he thinks senior management wants to hear, or even connive with his line manager to 'fix' the entries.
- The motivation to use reports is absent, either because line management and staff have not been educated in the value of reports to the company, or because they are not involved in using them to improve effectiveness. In other words, line management and staff have no ownership of the system. This lack of motivation may be a result of lack of strong line control of sales staff, such that a first line sales or branch manager feels free to disregard procedures, so long as he/she produces results. If overall, the company is seen to have a highly productive sales operation, the justification for detailed reporting may not be apparent.

- The data are asked for in retrospect, so recall is inaccurate. This applies particularly to the 'personal' factors mentioned above.
- The reports are produced too late to be of any practical use.

Implications

The implications of these points are as follows:

1. Information needed to generate the KPIs must, with few exceptions, be gathered as part of normal database marketing and sales operations. Most information activities should improve the specific marketing operation in question and be shown to do so to the marketing operators involved. This ensures that information is up-to-date and takes a mimimum of additional time to collect. Where other information is collected, this should be set as a separate task (e.g. a general questionnaire via telemarketing).
2. Staff involved in inputting information should be provided with rapid feedback which will help them improve their own effectiveness, and they should be trained to do so. They should also be involved in designing the reports they are to receive. This will help improve the relevance and usefulness of reports, and also create ownership.
3. Time/resource spent collecting, inputting and processing information must be controlled as in any other sales or marketing activity.
4. Line management must be trained to use reports. They should also input into report design, to ensure the reports give them the information they need. Ideally, they should be able to specify their own reports on-line.
5. Line management must be assessed partly or even principally through their performance according to the reports. If the reports are unable to provide critical KPIs to assess line management, they will probably fall into disuse. Reports and the input systems must be developed consistently with the line management culture of the company. If they are seen as 'over-controlling' relative to the culture, they are likely to be difficult to implement and use. KPIs are an aid to the management process, not a substitute for it.
6. Considerable resource needs to be devoted to preparing relevant, easily understood and rapidly available reports.

KPIs in detail

A database marketing system is in one sense the ideal mechanism for ensuring that all the aforementioned points are dealt with. Much of the information required is generated in the day to day running of the system. However, this may be the core of the problem – too much information may be available. This is why the idea of the marketer's workbench should be taken seriously. Many of the decisions made by the marketer at his workbench will be based on KPIs of one kind or another.

There is no limit to the numbers or types of KPIs that could be reported. They should be chosen so as to reflect the competitive needs of the business and the revenue and cost productivity of resources.

There is an almost infinite number of ratios, each producing slightly different insights. In many cases, the ratios will be second or third order (e.g. sales per customer type per product per area). These ratios all form part of the 'chain of productivity', any element of which may have some significance for management purposes. What is a KPI in one situation may not be a KPI in another – a slightly different ratio may need to be investigated. Indeed, pre-specifying KPIs ignores the fact that inspecting different reports and ratios leads to much learning as to which indicators actually are most important, which are helpful in diagnostic work, which only need to be reported by exception, etc. The appropriate policy is therefore to have pre-specified and automatically produced reports for most significant ratios, with other reports specifiable 'at the touch of a button'.

Note that many ratios used in marketing tend to be in terms of overall averages. Productivity analysis must be able to identify diminishing returns, for example, of extending a campaign to another market segment, of expanding telemarketing coverage, of increasing sales force numbers. This is because ratios are often used as indicators of whether it makes sense (in terms of expected returns) to expand or contract resource allocation to particular activities. For example, we might want to know the productivity of the weakest 10 per cent of sales staff, the likely lifetime values of the earliest 10 per cent of responders to a campaign, or the productivity of sales staff responsible for the 20 per cent of customers with highest volume of purchasing.

All indicators should be measured overall, by product and customer type where appropriate. Ratio indicators can be by call, enquiry, operator, salesperson, outlet, time, contact strategy, score, area, product, customer type as appropriate. Performance should be measured against plan and previous period where appropriate.

Below, we outline some examples of KPIs that can be used in measuring the effectiveness of a database marketing approach. Not all these would be used. The best policy is to adopt a hierarchy of indicators, those at the highest level of aggregation being used to assess overall marketing performance, and those at the lowest level being used to assess individual elements of the marketing process. The indicators given relate principally to what we call 'field marketing' – i.e. units in direct contact with customers. Some indication of how other marketing staff (e.g. product marketers and sector marketers) should be assessed is also given.

KPIs for field marketing (i.e. customer contact units)

These measures are of channel effectiveness. The most general measure for each channel is the projected lifetime value of customers wholly or completely managed through it.

CALLING SALES FORCE

Call rates	Cost
Closes	Order size
Lead conversion	Revenue and contribution
Share of customer business	Customer satisfaction
Customer loss prevention	Customer gain
Senior decision maker contacts	Sales/pre-sales surveys initiated
Target product mix	Target customer mix

TELEMARKETING

Dials	Call rate
Customer wait (autodial)	Call length
Non-phone time	Completed calls
Decision maker contacts	Contacts discussed with
Contacts advanced	Direct sales
Lead generation	Appointments
Invitations	Demonstrations
Quality of lead	Lead conversions
Cross-selling	Up-selling
Customer loss prevention	Customer gain
Customer satisfaction	Bad debt
Returns	Gone-aways
Target product mix	Target customer mix

RETAIL CHANNEL (for sales to consumer customers)
(Additional denominators for ratios – floor area and cost)

Inventory total	Stock turn
Stock-outs	Wastage
Cost of goods sold	Sales staff cost
Site cost	Merchandising cost
Fitting costs	Site costs
Achieved gross and net margin	Contribution
Traffic	Customer satisfaction
Leads generated	Returns
Target product mix	Target customer mix

SHOWROOMS (for sales to business customers)
(Additional denominators for ratios – floor area and cost)

Closes	Order size
Lead generation and conversion	Revenue and contribution
Revenue and contribution	Share of customer business
Customer satisfaction	Customer loss prevention
Customer gain	Customer wait
Decision maker contacts	Contacts discussed with

Contacts advanced
Invitations
Cross-selling
Sales staff cost
Merchandising/display cost
Target product mix

Further appointments made
Demonstrations
Up-selling
Site cost
Visit frequency/utilization
Target customer mix

SALES OFFICE (base for local sales staff, not purely telemarketing)
Enquiries handled
Order size
Revenue and contribution
Customer satisfaction
Customer gain
Call length
Completed calls
Lead generation
Invitations
Quality of lead
Cross-selling
Customer loss prevention
Customer satisfaction
Returns
Target customer mix

Orders processed
Lead conversion
Share of customer business
Customer loss prevention
Customer wait for query resolution
Non-phone time
Contacts advanced
Appointments
Demonstrations
Lead conversions
Up-selling
Customer gain
Bad debt
Target product mix

DIRECT ORDER
Outbound cost
Delivery cost
Total cost
Cross-leads generated
Bad debts
Target product mix
Damage in transit

Enquiry handling cost
Installation cost
Orders received
Returns
Gone aways
Target customer mix
Post-sales queries

All channels should be assessed in addition on:

Headcount
Allocation to key tasks

Sales and contribution productivity

Inventory
Matching to customer needs
Inventory turn
Obsolescence

Matching to product strategies
Launch provisioning

Revenue, contribution and profit
Size in relation to resources

The need for a clear policy framework

The financial aspects of database marketing can seem very complicated compared with the approach to, say, the advertising budgeting of many companies. But the disciplines described above are part of the new wave of total marketing accountability. However, marketing accountability requires more than statistics. It also requires a strong framework within which the accountability is exercised.

15 Marketing planning

Database marketing is to field sales what farming is to hunting or shooting. There are no quick returns to database marketing. Database marketers know better than any other marketers that:

- Customers who are contacted more buy more than those who are contacted less
- Customers who have bought more often will buy more often in the future
- Customers who have bought greater amounts will buy greater amounts in the future
- Customers who have bought more recently will buy more in the future.

All these statements refer to the future. They refer to how the customer base – the most important marketing asset – is going to deliver its value. Much of what we are doing in database marketing is managing future revenue streams and customer lifetime values. This is why it is essential to develop a coherent framework for managing database marketing campaigns. We have found the following distinctions helpful in creating the framework:

- *Strategic planning* – planning 3–5 years ahead for revenues, resources and costs and the strategies that underlie them. The main disciplines here are long range revenue and resource planning. The kinds of market information that we use here relate to long term customer loyalty, evolution of buying behaviour, long term changes in the media and distribution channel costs that make up contact strategy costs. For this kind of planning to be coherent, a relatively stable corporate plan is required.
- *Campaign planning* – an annual or quarterly plan for a series of campaigns,

155

whether tests or roll-outs. The main disciplines here are testing, forecasting and managing co-ordination across campaigns.

- *Campaign design* – the phase before the launch of each campaign, where inputs from a variety of agencies and management groups are brought together to create the design of a campaign and the plan for its implementation. The main management discipline required here is project management. The main information needed is on availability of the resources for planning and implementing the campaign.
- *Campaign execution and measurement* – starting with the launch of a campaign, early and constant measurement, allowing campaign modification if necessary, and continuing until the close of the campaign. The main disciplines required here are attention to detail in ensuring that every aspect of implementation has been dealt with. The main information needed is performance feedback from those responsible for all elements of the contact strategy and for final fulfilment.
- *Campaign reporting* – the final results of the campaign are reported and analysed, providing the basis for subsequent planning. Here, the main disciplines are statistical and analytical, with some creativity required to interpret reasons for success and failure.
- *Campaign library* – where the results of campaigns are archived.

Figure 15.1 shows how these concepts relate to each other.

The importance of commitment

Database marketing campaigns usually involve many people in the company. For example, a campaign aimed at stimulating sales through a direct sales force may involve central marketing staff, telemarketing staff, branch sales office staff, sales managers and sales staff. All these staff need to be committed to making the campaign successful. They also need to be well informed of the objectives of the campaign and their role within it, and informed in time. This means that detailed planning must be meticulous to achieve the best results.

Organizing for planning

In large, multi-product organizations, the degree of coordination required by database marketing may be difficult to achieve. A company moving towards using database marketing as the central plank of its marketing approach should consider whether its current planning processes are appropriate. The cross-product cross-sector nature of database marketing usually requires more coordination within their marketing and sales organizations than many companies are used to. It may be necessary to set up one or more new policy

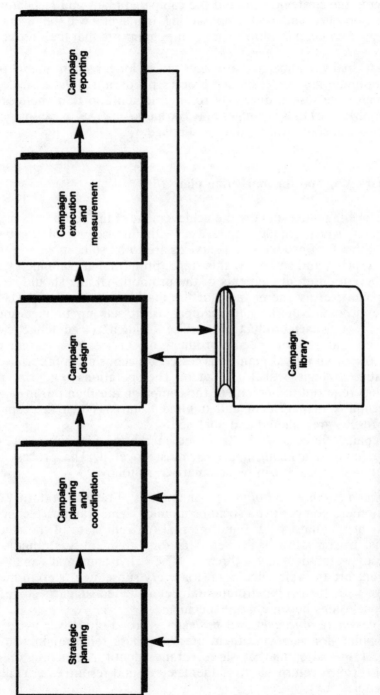

Figure 15.1: Marketing management process

bodies to agree the strategic plan and the campaign plans and to deal with any conflicts. As product and sector marketing managers will be users of the approach, they may need to form a user group, to ensure that their requirements are mutually agreed.

Given that many campaigns are not much longer than many ordinary marketing promotions, the planning process needs not only a strategic and annual element, but also a quarterly rolling element, so that changes can be incorporated. Many of these changes may be due to changes in campaigns based on test results, but some will be due to slippage.

Database marketing and the marketing plan

Database marketing must support the achievement of the company's marketing plan. The plan, which should be devised with intense use of the database, should establish which products and services are to be sold, in what quantities, to which customers, and so on. At this stage, promotional planning establishes what contribution different elements of the promotional mix should be.

The campaign plan is one element of the marketing plan. It selects specific products, services and markets for campaigns. It sets up timings and likely media for promoting each product and service. Using it as a guideline, campaign plans are then laid out for specific products or services. The target market, specified in the promotional plan, is accessed by choosing appropriate lists or media. Creative strategies will also be set up. The operations (e.g. print, mailing, telemarketing) required to implement the campaign are then put in place. The process of enquiry management and fulfilment starts. When the campaign is completed, results are collated and analysed.

Most companies have a well-established marketing planning process, with which the database marketing approach must dovetail. The process used by most marketing companies can be summarised as follows:

- *External and internal environment* – an analysis of relevant external (market and customer, competitive, socio-economic, demographic, technological, government, regulatory etc.) and internal (current state of the company – resources, organization, skills, etc.) factors, to identify strengths, weaknesses, opportunities and threats. The environmental analysis and conclusions are the reference point for every subsequent step in marketing planning, with further environmental detail added at each stage, as the policy conclusions become more specific.
- *Overall company objectives and strategies* – broad objectives and the main lines of policy for achieving them are set. These relate mainly to market presence (e.g. sales, market share, brand identity, franchise or image), financial (profits, return on investment, etc.), and resources or skills (technical, people, etc.).

- *Marketing objectives and strategies* – derived directly from company strategies, especially from those relating to market presence. From objectives are derived marketing strategies, which define the broad lines of marketing policy.
- *Marketing mix* – the detailed specification of marketing policies, including quantification of the outcomes of their implementation.
- *Marketing implementation and support* – the processes which ensure delivery of marketing policies and their results. They include planning, organization, targeting, incentives, controls.
- *Marketing achievement* – when the plan is put into effect, it must be monitored and controlled, with corrective actions being taken as necessary. The experience of implementation may lead to refinement of company and marketing objectives.

We now show how the database marketing approach integrates with this planning process. This analysis is not exhaustive, for reasons of space, but it does show how database marketing can drive the marketing process.

Internal and external environment

Realistic business and marketing plans are based on a thorough appreciation of what is going on today, inside and outside the company, and what is likely to go on in the future, under different policy assumptions. External environment factors of particular interest are customers (actual and potential), media and competitors (actual and potential). Other external factors which might be relevant include technology and legislation (e.g. Data and Consumer Protection Acts). 'Internal environment' refers to the company itself, its resources, people, direction and current policies.

This analysis is not just a compilation of facts, but an attempt to identify strengths and weaknesses (of the company, its brand and its present policies and resources), and thence single out opportunities to be captured and threats to be dealt with. The analysis is then put together with the needs of the owners of the business (and sometimes other interested parties e.g. employees, members) to arrive at a statement of feasible objectives.

The main environmental analysis tasks relevant to database marketing are information gathering and analysis in relation to customers and competition. Database marketing may eventually provide the main channel through which a company receives information about customer and prospect needs. Much of the information required may already be in the database. Information which is lacking can be generated using database marketing techniques, either in research campaigns or as part of testing or roll-out of campaigns.

However, in many cases, the most significant advantage of using database marketing is that it reduces the amount of general market information required before taking marketing decisions. For example, instead of determining a totally fixed marketing mix before the launch of a new product, different contact strategies may be implemented, depending on information gathered during the marketing process. Testing using database marketing techniques provides very valuable insights into a company's strengths and weaknesses as revealed by market behaviour.

Database marketing can provide a valuable addition to information on competitors. In some cases, questionnaires may be used to establish ownership or use of competitive products, perception of and attitudes to them.

Company objectives and strategies

Typical company objectives might be:

- To achieve a particular rate of asset growth
- To build and sustain return on assets, as an objective in its own right and also as support to the growth of assets.

The contribution of database marketing to the above two objectives is mainly to help make more productive use of marketing assets (e.g. customers, brand franchise). This is done partly by deriving higher revenues from them (i.e. higher asset turn), partly by defending the customer base more effectively, and partly by reducing marketing costs.

- To enhance the perceived value of company shares. Here, database marketing techniques can be used to influence shareholders and opinion formers.

Marketing objectives and strategies

Typical marketing objectives and strategies might be:

- To penetrate existing customers in depth – by maximizing the benefits provided to them, by multiplying the revenue streams arising from provision of these benefits, and by increasing customer loyalty. The use of database marketing is in identifying the needs of existing customers, providing the most cost-effective route for meeting these needs, and devising and implementing campaigns which will produce the desired revenue streams at the right profitability. It can also help through campaigns specifically designed to reinforce customer loyalty.
- To increase the size of the long term customer base, using database marketing to identify potential new customers who are most likely to remain loyal in the long run, and to devise and implement campaigns aimed at maintaining their loyalty.
- To reduce marketing costs, using database marketing to provide cost-effective channels for communication to reach target customers, for customers

to access the company, and for products and services to be delivered to customers.

- To create appropriate positioning and branding with all customers, using database marketing to provide research information as input into positioning and branding studies, and to deliver communication to customers to reinforce positioning and branding.

Marketing mix, implementation and support

The main aspects which use of database marketing can influence are as follows:

- Identification of needs of and potential future customers. Our earlier analysis on marketing assets (brands and customers) indicates that the logically prior question for most companies is 'what are the needs of customers whose needs we can serve with some competitive advantage?', and not 'what is the market for our products?'. Analysis of the customer database should provide the answer.
- Identification of the full range of products that can be marketed so as to fulfil agreed marketing strategies, given the needs identified above. Database analysis can be used to identify market potential, while testing can be used to gauge response to concepts and for test marketing.
- Ensuring that the right customers are actually reached with the right products at the right time, with the right offer. The roles of database marketing here are to match individual customers to the target market profile, to test the variety of marketing mixes (offers and contact strategies) and to provide the applications to deliver those mixes. Further development of a company's database marketing system may be needed to achieve this. For example, a company using its system only for mail and inbound telemarketing may need to add outbound telemarketing applications.
- Establishment of reporting and financial systems to provide ways of measuring performance against sales and profit targets for different markets and products. Financial and market criteria for evaluating campaigns can be set using database marketing ratios. Performance can be evaluated using data generated during campaign implementation.

Setting out the plan

Setting out the marketing plan using a database marketing approach is not too different from normal marketing planning approaches. However, the constant feedback of information from campaigns provides opportunities to improve the marketing mix rapidly. Attention must therefore be given to the phasing of the implementation of the marketing plan. If we assume that main target markets have been identified and marketing strategies agreed for them, we can best plan the phasing of our database marketing policy by combining three simple management techniques.

- A spreadsheet for financials, to indicate the likely outcomes of the various campaigns which we might run in our target markets
- A project management sheet (its periods aligned with the spreadsheet), to indicate the main decisions and activities (research, campaigns, resource allocation)
- A flow diagram to represent the logical ordering of the plan.

16 Campaigns and their design

The campaign is central to database marketing. It is sometimes very simple, involving the use of a single medium to make only one communication within a short period (e.g. one mail shot sent out over a week). But some campaigns involve a variety of media, combined in several different contact strategies, each chosen after testing several alternatives. Campaigns work on the principle of concentration, domination, repetition. We choose target customers and concentrate our communication on them. This means two-way communication, so we are receiving especially well too! We thereby counter competitive actions during the period in which we are repeating our communication.

Database marketing lends itself well to campaigns. We can use the database to focus every element of our marketing power. But this depends on making the right decisions on:

- Targeting – whom we talk to
- Timing – when and how often we talk to them
- The offer – why they should respond (i.e. because of relevance to their needs)
- Creative – how we persuade them to respond.

Targeting

The theme of targeting runs strongly through this book, and especially so in Chapter 11. For the purposes of this chapter, the most important message is that targeting is not a question of looking for customers for a product. Rather, it is looking for customers with needs which the company can satisfy. When these customers have been identified, we can devise campaigns which will allow these customers to develop their relationship with the company further. This may involve no purchasing, or the purchasing of several products.

Timing

One principle of database marketing is that the customer should be approached when he is most likely to buy. For example, peak buying of consumer durables is at time of household formation or after a house move. House buyers go through a process which makes it possible for us to target them. They take out mortgages, engage the services of certain professionals, buy certain magazines and read certain pages in the newspaper. There are times of year when it is inappropriate to approach customers, perhaps because they are about to go on holiday, or because they have their minds on other things (e.g. seasonal festivities!).

The timing of a campaign must also be closely coordinated with that of other campaigns, to prevent over-communicating with customers, or confusing them with conflicting messages. We also need to watch the timing of competitive campaigns, to avoid our own campaigns being 'drowned out'.

The offer

The offer is a critical part of every campaign. It is similar to the pressure that a salesman can bring to bear in a face-to-face call. The objectives of making an offer include:

- To get or focus attention
- To overcome inertia and stimulate interest
- To give a reason why the prospect should respond immediately
- To make the response more significant, i.e. make people buy more, by heightening the value perceived by the customer

There are many ways of creating an offer. Here are a few examples:

- Bundling several products or services together
- Limiting the offer to a given period or to customers responding before a certain date – this must be stated very clearly, to prevent later misunderstanding
- Incentives to attend exhibitions, sales seminars, retail outlets, by announcement of small 'give-aways'. Care must be taken to ensure that incentives are not personal inducements for staff (e.g. public service) for whom this would be inappropriate.

The ideal offer has the greatest perceived value to the customer, yet costs the least. High quality customer information helps us to define the appropriate offer for our target market. We must take into account the margin available to us to cover our marketing costs, and the complexity of the sales process. In a campaign for a low margin product, a good offer is one which brings in leads of such quality that the investment in further qualifying is low and the conversion rate is high.

One advantage of database marketing is that different offers can be tested relatively quickly. Pricing can also be tested. Higher prices with extra added value may be tested against lower prices.

The creative element

'Creative' relates to how a given offer is made to a given audience, with a given timing. In mail shots, it is the execution of the brief in copy and pictorial elements and how the mail shot is packaged. In a telephone campaign, it covers scripts and questionnaires.

A successful creative element depends on a clear brief, covering:

- The product or service – what it is and does, what is new or special about it (features, shapes, colours, quality, speed, functionality), what it competes with/replaces, its advantages and benefits for target customers
- The target market – who are natural prospects are for it and who could be persuaded to buy it
- What can be said about it – guarantees, value for money, proof, testimonials, topicality, constraints, taboos, sacred cows.

A good creative element usually follows the advertising rules of attracting attention, capturing and developing interest, engendering and enhancing desire, fostering conviction and asking for and spurring to action.

Most marketing companies work very hard to achieve consistency of image. A clear image, consistently portrayed and built up over the years, becomes a very strong marketing asset. It makes customers familiar with a company, and preconditions them to accept communication. The image that a company projects supports its positioning and branding. All database marketing communications must therefore support the image and be consistent with the positioning and branding of the company. At the same time, the desired image itself should be tested frequently to ensure that it is likely to deliver the right business results.

Campaign planning

In a large, multi-product company, the introduction of database marketing can lead to a confused and unstructured approach to customers caused by a free-for-all among marketing managers with different responsibilities but with similar target markets. We therefore must ensure co-ordination of the schedule of campaigns as soon as marketing opportunities are identified.

A company with a good marketing database also needs to ensure that it is getting the most out of it. It therefore needs a structured and comprehensive process for identifying marketing opportunities from the database. This too must be an objective right at the start of campaign development.

The initial aim is to get an estimate of the revenue and contribution for potential campaigns. Sample databases are extracted from the database for identification of target segments and simulation of different campaigns. Individual prospects can be identified and ranked to give a sales prediction. Alternative contact strategies (frequency, timing, media, etc.) can be set up to identify the best way of reaching customers. Then, trial extracts can be run against the sample databases to assess degree of clash between campaigns and hence potential over contacting of customers. This process is likely to be iterative. A large number of potential campaigns may be identified, placed on a campaign shortlist, and re-evaluated using a variety of criteria (e.g. strategic need, profit).

A database marketing system enables us to segment and accurately target our markets, ensure delivery of communication to our target customers, and handle responses from these customers professionally. Communications on behalf of different marketing groups (e.g. product marketing, sector marketing, area marketing) must be properly co-ordinated. The output of a campaign coordination system is a schedule of all planned campaigns. It gives details on each campaign (e.g. targeting, timing) and can be used to inform all relevant parties and enable them to plan their activities and resourcing more accurately. This ensures that customers are not alienated by being swamped by a multiplicity of apparently unrelated promotional material, with the associated risk of damage to company image.

The plan should be revised frequently to reflect changes in the business environment, such as competitive activity, non-availability of products, new products, or the need to promote slow moving products. Enquiry handling organizations (for example, telemarketing) must be able to ensure the availability of resources (trained operators, workstations and lines); fulfilment services must be geared up to respond to customer enquiries, and computer operations must have sufficient resources to handle the volume of work.

The development of marketing plans might be carried out as follows:

1. Campaign development
2. Campaign coordination
3. Campaign scheduling

Campaign development

- Marketing priorities are determined within the overall context of business and marketing plans. The objectives and nature of each proposed campaign are outlined.
- Different marketing groups (e.g. product or brand managers, sector marketing managers) input information about their priorities and intentions into the general strategy development process and into any groups formulating overall policy, and the latter also provide information of this kind to different marketing groups.
- Each marketing group outlines its overall campaign intentions. The objectives and nature of each proposed campaign are outlined.

Campaign co-ordination

Marketing groups meet to identify areas for potential cooperation or of possible overlap or conflict. They coordinate their broad intentions and priorities are agreed for the coming year. (This might involve several stages of draft and comment.) The specific tasks include:

- Establishing a campaign development plan, including preparation of a work plan and responsibilities with target dates for each task
- Establishing a campaign database, from campaign objectives, through market coverage and contact strategy (including variation for different priority enquiries), to implementation details (e.g. offer, media, list)
- Administering and controlling campaign development, via checklist-based support for briefing meetings, report chasing for all participants, and preparation of weekly status reports
- Refining the campaign plan, by modifying the campaign database according to subsequent decisions
- Sending campaign set-up information to the main database system.

Campaign scheduling

- Marketing groups confirm their individual campaign requirements in the context of the agreed statement of intentions. These are summarized and entered into the campaign coordination system to provide a basis for developing outline campaign schedules. Standard data entry forms should be used, to specify the treatment each marketing group expects to run (nature, timing, etc.)
- Outline campaign schedules for each marketing group are then produced by the co-ordination system
- The overall schedule is reviewed and priorities reassigned if necessary. This may include assignment of campaign treatments to time slots, prioritization

of treatments in each time slot (if clashes exist), preparation of the overall schedule of top priority treatments sequenced by campaign, cross referenced to lower priority treatment activity where appropriate

- Discussions between marketing groups take place to finalize campaign timing, maximize opportunitities for cooperation and avoid clashes or overlaps
- Revisions to initial plans are fed back into the system and revised schedules are prepared.

The details required for each campaign are:

- Objectives
- Business justification (contribution, revenue, etc.)
- Product
- Description of the offer
- Target market and segments
- Whether test or roll-out
- Fulfilment requirements
- Coverage
- Resource availability – to handle enquiries and fulfilment
- Start and end dates roll-out and test
- Start and end dates
- Media
- Likely volumes
- Response mechanism

These data should be used to allocate priorities to different campaigns.

Implementing a campaign coordination system requires the adoption of a closely structured planning timetable, with clear deadlines for the input of information and for the carrying out of all actions.

Campaign management

Once we have decided to go ahead with a campaign, we must ensure that it is implemented correctly and on time. This is the function of a campaign management system. It controls the process by which a campaign is taken from a paper description through to implementation. The main components of such a system are:

- Agency briefing and response
- Media/list selection
- Campaign detail finalization

Campaign management is similar to conventional project management and is based on reverse scheduling from the end of the planned campaign. The reverse schedule is based on standard task lists and checklists and on normal lead times for completion of each task. The management plan includes a series of target dates or milestones. These normally relate to specific outputs, such as draft scripts and copy being available for management review and approval, and list extracts being completed. The system enables all parties involved in implementing a campaign to enquire about the current status of a campaign against these milestones.

Agency briefing

The campaign management process starts here. Well before a campaign's scheduled start date, an agency briefing is agreed and the agency is given the go ahead to start work. The development of the brief is a cooperative exercise between the company and the agency. The agency responds to the brief, in the form of a proposal, which includes:

- Suggested creative executions (including tests)
- Media proposals
- Forecast response/order rates
- Proposed contact strategies
- Creative production schedule

Following agreement to the proposal, production schedules are issued.

Media/list selection

Before a campaign starts, a meeting between involved marketing staff and agencies should be held, to confirm:

- Media choice and detailed specification (including tests)
- Target market details (including tests)
- List characteristics and coverage

If the campaign requires the use of media, planning and buying commences. If it requires direct mail or telemarketing, the company begins the detailed analysis and list selection process. Following this meeting, media/list schedules will be issued.

Campaign finalization

Before campaign start, a meeting is held between marketing staff, agencies and relevant marketing service functions (telemarketing, fulfilment) to confirm:

- Enquiry management response scripts
- Fulfilment pack(s) and items
- Contact strategies (telemarketing scripts, etc.)

- Campaign treatments (tests of creative, list/media, geographic areas, market segments, offers)
- Postal imprints
- Manpower resources (e.g. telemarketing teams)
- Stock availability

Database marketing campaigns demand a high degree of cooperation between several internal departments and between these departments and various external suppliers of expertise or services. Database marketing therefore depends on good briefs for each department and supplier, including the data and policy statements (objectives, target markets, etc.) required by those working on campaign development or implementation. These might include problem definition, overall market situation, statements of objectives and strategies, competitive situation, customer behaviour, target markets, current plans, budgets available, constraints, the chief benefit of the product or service, details of other products or services which may be promoted with the product, research summary, and the main message to be transmitted.

The main brief becomes a source brief for a variety of other briefs to the many in-house and out-house suppliers. In-house briefs may be targeted at any of the following:

- Clerical staff
- Field and office sales staff
- Receptionists
- The mailroom
- The warehouse
- Other marketing staff
- Internal telemarketing agency/department
- Internal enquiry handling facility

External briefs may be targeted at:

- The direct marketing agency
- The advertising agency
- Exhibition contractors
- Promotional agency
- Designers
- Writers
- The printers
- The telemarketing agency
- Fulfilment house.

The mechanisms described in this and the previous chapter for integrating database marketing into the marketing planning process of a company may seem a little ponderous. But without a very structured approach to the introduction of the new discipline of database marketing, a company would risk some degree of chaos, with a multiplicity of campaigns being targeted at the wrong customers, and with internal staff and agencies not being managed so as to deliver what is required of them.

17 Marketing accountability

The adoption of database marketing can change the way a company markets its products and this can affect how a company organizes its marketing. However, the exact way in which the marketing organization should change is not clear. There are few precedents. Publishing companies and others who use direct mail as their sole channel and run their marketing entirely through database marketing are not an appropriate model for a company which has a large sales force or a chain of retail outlets, or which has factories to keep running. Uncertainty as to which organizational model to follow is compounded by the following factors:

- Database marketing uses a variety of very specialized skills and techniques, many of which are new to marketers.
- The overall approach to planning, controlling and managing database marketing is radically different from classic brand planning or industrial marketing.
- The experience and background of database marketers is very often different from those of their marketing colleagues.
- There has been no serious effort to integrate the disciplines of database marketing into marketing training, whether in business schools or in company programmes. This means that even very well trained marketers come ill prepared for its disciplines.
- Database marketing may seem to outsiders to be wanting to set up a business within a business, in relation to how it goes about planning its policies, designs and implements its systems, carries out campaigns and uses distribution channels. This can create problems of perceived threat within the traditional marketing and sales organization.

- Non-database marketers persist in seeing it as a solution to tactical problems. This is part of the heritage of first phase direct marketing, as described in Chapter 6. This heritage takes some time to overcome.
- Insistence on accountability for marketing actions and results can create a threat with managers responsible for large marketing budgets who feel that they are not using them as productively as they could.
- The lack of track record when the approach is first adopted, combined with the high initial investment with no short term results, makes database marketing very vulnerable in its infancy in a company.
- The economies of scale in database marketing imply a high degree of centralization, at least for some aspects of campaigns. This may cause alienation in a company with decentralized marketing or sales.
- If database marketing is seen as a support to tactical activity, database marketers are not allowed to influence strategic thinking. Therefore, strategies which exploit the full range of database marketing techniques are not adopted. Thus, database marketing is never thought of early enough in the policy planning process. A vicious circle becomes established.
- The problems of establishing database marketing can lead to impatience on the part of experts who have been hired to establish it. They leave, and are replaced either by new experts who may have to begin the cycle of influencing again, or by other marketing staff who do not understand or sympathize with the approach.

This list of problems may create a degree of pessimism about integration. However, the longer term prognosis is good, because in every area of marketing, techniques are being developed for increasing the measurability of the results of marketing initiatives. This applies to above the line advertising, sales promotion, retail point of sale, retail design, sales force incentives, and so on. The notion of measurability and accountability is therefore making strong headway in most marketing communities. This, combined with the rising cost of non-targeted media, provides fertile ground for database marketing to take root and grow. But it still leaves us with the problem of how to integrate it into the marketing organization.

If database marketing is to find its place in the organization, we must recognize one of the fundamental findings of the history of organizational analysis when applied to all marketing. This is that the best marketing companies are not necessarily those with the largest marketing departments. The best are those where marketing is established as a way of life. In such companies, many managers may have marketing expertise, irrespective of their job titles. A marketing services department may supply these managers with specific disciplines and support, but the custodians of the marketing approach are all the managers in a company.

However, in many companies, marketing *is* driven by the marketing department, which has taken control of or at a minimum has a commanding influence over all the decision making processes which affect customers (e.g. product design and development, inventory, physical distribution, marketing channels). Database marketing can live with either of these approaches. It requires specialist technical support, but it also requires absorption of its disciplines into the way of life of most functions.

Much of the work carried out so far in developing database marketing systems has been on the development of concepts (e.g. database design), systems (e.g. fulfilment) and applications (e.g. telemarketing). This work has focused on:

- What we are trying to get our customers to do
- What systems and procedures we need to implement to make sure that our customers get what we have promised them.

Less work has been done on how to help our staff work with this new way of doing business, involving working at the level of perceptions, understanding and needs. In short, we need to market database marketing internally. We are asking our staff to accept new marketing disciplines and new systems disciplines.

The new marketing disciplines for, say, the brand or product manager, are direct contact with individual customers and a relationship with the customer that is so strong that it reinforces and develops branding and forms the basis for increasingly profitable campaigns. The new systems disciplines relate to the gathering, holding, analysis and exploitation of individual customer data, rather than aggregated or market research data. They include the management of large databases, some variables of which are not in the company's control. The database must be updated in a variety of ways, normally after every contact with the customer. Marketing policies are viewed as applications which run off the main database and system. Applications are designed with much stronger input relating to customer needs. For sales forces, perhaps used to a relatively unstructured but, in their view, creative and motivating dialogue with customers, database marketing involves working in a more structured way with customers, as part of a coherent contact strategy. Activity is managed more closely, but also more directly in response to customer needs rather than the needs of the sales force and their management.

Staff are coming up against new disciplines with increasing frequency as the database marketing approach extends outwards from classical direct marketing users towards fully integrated manufacturing or retailing businesses. This creates new sets of users, influencers and beneficiaries, who need to get to grips with the ideas and disciplines of database marketing.

Many systems are implemented in a relatively short time, perhaps over three to five years. This may sound a long time, but not for a fully comprehensive system. It is a very short time in the development cycle of a company's overall marketing approach. Most companies change their marketing approach very slowly, over many years. The concept of brand management took many decades to evolve to its current state. The disciplines of account management take years to instil in an organization accustomed to making most of its sales through prospecting for new customers.

We need to recognize how long it takes to change, and also how widespread is the effect of the change. It affects staff in marketing, sales, service, systems, customer administration, finance, distribution, inventory management and of course general management. It may imply new organization structures and pay scales, with implications for recruitment, motivation and training. Staff find themselves working with different groups of individuals and different external suppliers. Handling this kind of change takes time – to plan, motivate, influence and train.

Organizational analysis

The best starting point for organizational analysis is to identify how a database marketing approach will affect the main management groups involved in marketing. A database marketing system will have many different users in a company. In what follows, we define a number of groups – product management, product marketing, customer marketing, marketing services and general marketing management. We suggest how their accountabilities might be divided and the consequent kind of use they might make of the system. Figure 17.1 provides an overview of accountabilities.

Product management

The responsibilities of product management are:

- Identifying customer needs relevant to products. Some information as to which customers' needs are to be satisfied (i.e. target markets) is drawn from strategic marketing plans (the responsibility of general marketing management), but much comes from customer marketing and secondarily from product marketing (see below for definitions)
- Technically specifying products, to ensure profitable marketability, taking into account customer needs and competition. Maintaining the specification throughout the product's life to ensure continued competitive marketability
- Planning and achieving product availability in the markets for which the product is specified (including ensuring that it can be supported technically, before and after the sale, once out in the market place)
- Ensuring the availability of all the information needed to carry out the function and liaising with all relevant functions to ensure the achievement of the above objectives.

Product management is likely to require aggregated reports from the marketing database, relating to customer needs and behaviour (especially purchase patterns). Occasionally, they might wish to investigate some characteristics of

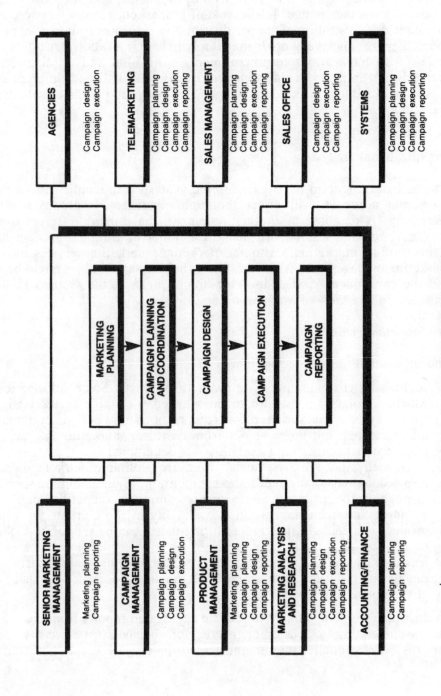

DATABASE MARKETING

SENIOR MARKETING MANAGEMENT
Marketing planning
Campaign reporting

CAMPAIGN MANAGEMENT
Campaign planning
Campaign design
Campaign execution

PRODUCT MANAGEMENT
Marketing planning
Campaign planning
Campaign design
Campaign reporting

MARKETING ANALYSIS AND RESEARCH
Campaign planning
Campaign design
Campaign execution
Campaign reporting

ACCOUNTING/FINANCE
Campaign planning
Campaign reporting

MARKETING PLANNING

CAMPAIGN PLANNING AND COORDINATION

CAMPAIGN DESIGN

CAMPAIGN EXECUTION

CAMPAIGN REPORTING

AGENCIES
Campaign design
Campaign execution

TELEMARKETING
Campaign planning
Campaign design
Campaign execution
Campaign reporting

SALES MANAGEMENT
Campaign planning
Campaign design
Campaign execution
Campaign reporting

SALES OFFICE
Campaign design
Campaign execution
Campaign reporting

SYSTEMS
Campaign planning
Campaign design
Campaign execution
Campaign reporting

Figure 17.1: Involvement of different parts of the organization

individual customers in detail. They will need to use the system to provide volume forecasts, based on test campaigns.

Product marketing or brand management

The responsibilities of product marketing or brand management are:

- Marketing a product of a given technical specification.
- Obtaining and analysing information required to support its marketing e.g. information on how to identify and reach customers for the product.
- Devising plans to market them (positioning, branding, pricing, promotion, sales messages, distribution channels, pre and post-sales service and support) competitively and meet company objectives (financial, market, etc.).
- Implementing or helping implement some aspects of these plans (e.g. pricing, preparation of promotional campaigns).
- Recommending or determining modifications in product specification or design to enhance marketability.
- Providing tactical support to assist field sales and distribution channels to market the product.

The last two roles are often combined. They are best seen separated in multinational companies with truly international products (e.g. complex engineering products, such as vehicles, machine tools and computers). In such cases, product management 'sits' near the designated production and/or design centre for the product and channels marketing input into the product design process. Such international product managers often have the additional function of targeting national product marketers to achieve particular sales targets, based on market information provided by the national operating units (not necessarily through the product marketing staff).

The dividing line between the product manager and the product marketer is that the product manager delivers ('buys') the product for the product marketer to market. But there is usually some fuzziness at the border, with the product manager becoming involved in product marketing, and vice versa. However, the main difference is clear – the product manager delivers the product for the company, and the product marketer takes the product on from there.

Product marketing staff are likely to use the database marketing information in a similar way to product managers, and for every aspect of campaign planning and follow through to implementation and campaign close for their individual products. They require aggregated reports, but probably in more detail. They will use the database marketing system to create and implement campaigns for their products, subject to consistency with other campaigns.

Customer marketing

The responsibilities of customer marketing are:

- Identifying the product and service needs of specific groups of customers in relation to all products actually supplied and potentially suppliable by the company.
- Identifying the needs of specific groups of customers concerning the relationship with the company.
- Ensuring that all products supplied are presented to the customer appropriately (branding, marketing communications, pricing over the range, distribution channels, selling), meeting the needs of customers and the company.

In all but the smallest companies, each member of customer marketing staff will be responsible for a subset of the company's customers, just as a product manager is responsible for one or more products out of a range. Customer marketing has responsibility for channel policy and implementation and looks after all cross-product marketing. It is therefore heavily involved in the determination of field marketing policy and in ensuring its implementation.

Customer marketing will use the approach in a similar way to product marketing. The main exception will be their extensive involvement in contact strategy planning because of their accountability for distribution channel policy.

Field marketing

The responsibility of field marketing is:

- Implementing the relationship with the customer, meeting customer and company objectives (it therefore includes all owned channels – the field sales force, the sales office, walk-in channels and direct order, as well as those managing third party channels).

Field marketing is also responsible for achieving product targets. Some field marketing staff (e.g. sales or support staff) may be specialized by product group if not by individual product. Such staff are defined as field product marketing. In a consumer goods company, this is equivalent to having a dedicated product rep.

The dividing line between customer marketing and field marketing is the slightly fuzzy one of policy and implementation. The skills required are very different. Field marketing should be more strongly sales oriented, and rich in skills of dealing with individual customers. Customer marketing should be rich in the skills of analysing customers and working out how best to structure short, medium and long term relationships with them, over the whole marketing mix. Many branded consumer goods companies ignored for years the need for customer marketing, instead concentrating on product (brand) marketing. This led to a situation in which their retailer or trade marketing policies were in control of the sales (field marketing) operation. Relationships with retailers became essentially tactical, which in some cases allowed the balance of power to swing in the retailer's favour.

Field marketing management will use the database marketing system most intensively for actually managing contacts with customers and assessing their effectiveness from marketing, financial and quality perspectives.

General marketing management

The responsibilities of general marketing management are:

- Ensuring that the needs of customers and the company are balanced so as to create success in the short and long term, by allocating resources appropriately, by deciding between options and by making trade-offs.
- Ensuring that marketing systems and processes exist to contribute to the above (e.g. databases, planning process, order entry).
- Managing relationships with other functions and the company as a whole appropriately, and in particular ensuring that the customer/marketing orientation pervades the company.

General marketing management should use a database marketing system as the foundation stone for their general marketing policy, from revenue stream analysis through to implementing relationships with customers. All marketing policies should be evaluated using data drawn from the system, most of them generated through testing.

Marketing services

The responsibility of marketing services is:

- Providing research, analytical, planning, process, system and implementation expertise to support all other marketing functions. This includes expertise in implementing those elements of the marketing mix, such as pricing and marketing communications, which are required for both customer and product marketing.

Marketing services are likely to use the database marketing system as a source of research information on every marketing topic. They should also be heavily involved in analysing test results.

The marketing services area is the ideal location for database marketing technical expertise. They are used to the customer/supplier relationship with marketing staff. However, in some companies they would need to be much more proactive than currently in order to get the most out of database marketing. This is because they may be conditioned to a reactive role in meeting marketers' requests, rather than the proactive role that they would need to take in everything from strategic planning, through to campaign planning and implementation. If this role is not taken up, marketing services departments risk being undermined by the database marketing approach. Research derived data will be supplanted by customer transaction data. Sales forecasts based on extrapolation of general past performance will be replaced by forecasts based upon campaign tests.

The database marketing centre

In companies with established marketing departments, there will normally be a fairly well accepted approach to marketing analysis, decision making and implementation. This approach will be embodied in the marketing planning process, and in the organizational structure and job definitions and accountabilities of marketing staff. The approach may follow the 'brand management' model of many consumer goods companies, the business planning – marketing services – sales force model of many industrial product companies, or the HQ planning – branch or operations unit planning model of many service organizations.

Adopting the database marketing approach will introduce a new set of disciplines, needing specialist support, perhaps through the establishment of a database marketing centre. This centre would provide the marketing, computing and statistical expertise required to support and train marketers. It might be part of the marketing services operation, as recommended earlier.

The costs of such a centre depend on its size and speed of development, but also on how much of the marketing process (campaign design, development and implementation) and systems work (database and computing facility design, development and implementation) the company wishes to carry out in-house. Since nearly all the services required are available on a contract basis (e.g. systems consultancy and implementation, database management, campaign design and fulfilment), a company's speed and extent of adoption of database marketing is only limited by the availability of management to coordinate their use and the funding required.

We would never recommend contracting the operation out entirely – no company should contract out its strategic marketing development. But we would recommend most companies to contract out some of the most expensive items, at least initially. These include database holding and management, much of campaign design, and fulfilment. Contracting out provides experience which is essential in moving a company up its database marketing learning curve. It also allows database marketing to justify itself before heavy investments are made.

Staff skills

Database marketing requires the introduction of many new skills, ranging from strong computer disciplines, such as database creation and management, through to applications disciplines such as telemarketing and direct mail.

In large conventional marketing departments, staff understanding of the marketing process is often limited to their area of responsibility. Market researchers understand techniques of market research, but may understand little about the factors which determine the success of their company's products. Brand managers may know their brands inside out, but understand little about trade marketing. In the new, evolving disciplines of database marketing, the risk of this over-specialization is greater, particularly if staff concerned have the responsibility of implementing a rapidly growing database and a correspondingly rapidly growing volume of database marketing campaigns.

The consequence of such specialization is that some campaigns may not exploit all the features of the database and the system which manages it, and may over-use one application relative to others. The solution is to pay close attention to internal communication and training. A variety of solutions are available – here are some examples:

- Holding briefing sessions for staff, delivered either by the company's own specialists or by external suppliers (e.g. direct marketing and telemarketing agencies)
- Creation of some form of regular bulletin, updating all marketing staff on developments in different areas. If the marketing department is fully computerized, this can be done electronically
- Evaluation of the breadth and depth of knowledge of each member of the marketing department and provision of a tailored training programme to bring all members of the department up to a common level of skill.

If database marketing is being introduced to a company through a database marketing centre, then the 'customers' of the centre (e.g. marketing staff with responsibility for particular products, brands, market sectors) will need to be similarly informed and trained if they are to exploit database marketing appropriately. Without this, the centre's workload will be very high – they will be providing on the job training to their customers while trying to make and implement policy. The need for such training must be communicated to senior 'customer' management, and a structured approach adopted to identifying individuals who need the training, and providing it.

Account management

If a database marketing centre is established, a management structure must be set up to ensure that all the database marketing disciplines are integrated to create and implement effective campaigns for 'internal customers'. This requires the use of 'account management' disciplines similar to those used in the sale and implementation of complex projects. Account management must be combined with project management, to ensure that each project is delivered on time to customers, at the right quality. They must spend much of their time working with customers to ensure in-depth understanding of needs and quality implementation of database marketing. Account managers must manage their customers proactively, especially if database marketing disciplines are new to the company. To perform this task, they require the appropriate backing, resources (especially time), skills and management structure.

In a large company, it is arguable that these account managers should be full time, and not double their role with some other responsibility. Careful thought must be given to the grouping and allocation of internal customers to account managers – ideally the customers with the most similar needs should be grouped under the same account manager.

If account managers are to work with customers to ensure coordination of campaigns, implying some customers being asked to defer or forego campaigns, they will need the support of a coherent database marketing plan for principal product groups and market sectors, agreed beforehand with the appropriate internal customers. This should be an output of the campaign coordination system used by the company, in which the account managers must be closely involved. Because account managers need to act as both supporters of the coordinated database marketing plan and advocates of their customers, they should probably report to a sort of senior account manager, equivalent in seniority to the most senior 'functional' marketing managers.

The account manager's job is to see the process of coordinating campaigns from the internal customer's point of view and ensure that the database marketing centre's process meets customer needs as well as overall company needs. To help them see things from the customer's viewpoint, account managers should be trained in handling customers. Their expertise in database systems or database marketing will not normally qualify them well in this area. This training should cover everything from communicating (e.g. strategy) to customers, through to understanding and influencing customers and dealing with objections.

Project management is a discipline in its own right. Many marketing and systems staff are not used to working to the full disciplines of project management and using all the management tools available to help them. They need to be provided with these tools (e.g. computerized project management systems) and be trained to use them.

The role and accountabilities of account managers should be specified carefully and published for the benefit of customers and database marketing centre staff. All internal customers and staff should understand the nature of this accountability and their role in it. They should also understand clearly the nature of the database marketing process and the steps required to make it succeed.

The needs of internal customers, expressed in their marketing plans and in the briefs they give to the database marketing centre, are changing constantly. However, if the centre is kept informed of their needs, it will be better able to respond to them. It might help here if internal customers provide briefings to the centre, to stimulate its thinking as to how to meet customer needs.

18 The staff dimension

Database marketing brings many benefits to to a company's customers and to its marketing and sales staff. It is hard to be be precise about the impact of the system on staff, for various reasons:

1. Database marketing approaches evolve quite quickly, as more features, facilities and applications are added.
2. As the approach is developed, more and more use is made of it, involving more and more company staff. The disciplines of database marketing become more widely accepted. Many marketing and sales staff learn how to use it. The speed with which the learning takes place and with which the exploitation becomes effective will vary.
3. Marketing and sales organizations are likely to change, as market needs change, and as new ways of organizing to exploit the facilities of database marketing are discovered.

The above notwithstanding, we have a good general idea of how database marketing affects staff. In the following section, we give some examples of the likely impact on different categories of marketing and sales staff.

Implications for marketing communications staff

The role of the marketing communications manager changes significantly with the arrival of database marketing. The nature of this change can best be appreciated if you consider how important communications is in all marketing – however that communication is achieved, whether by media advertisement, telephone, salesperson, the retail outlet, the exhibition, the mail shot or any of the other media available. A database marketing approach radically improves the effectiveness of communication, but also requires that marketing communication be very closely coordinated with the rest of the marketing mix.

One of the distinguishing features of database marketing is that it requires close coordination between many different staff, from those who handle enquiries through to those who sell, deliver and install products, and provide after-sales support. The brief to internal staff must be very comprehensive if the campaign is to run smoothly.

Another implication of the high internal involvement is that, compared to above the line work, more of the costs and benefits will arise internally. The benefits consist of time saved (e.g. by sales staff), reduced advertising budgets, and the like. The costs include outbound communication, briefing internal staff, dealing with higher volumes of enquiries and of putting lower priority customers on the back burner. The more accurate the targeting, the higher the internal costs relative to the external costs.

A database marketing approach provides the company with better ways of planning marketing communications and for measuring the return on investment in marketing communications, so the degree of accountability of the marketing communications manager will rise.

All this assumes that the marketing communications manager takes on some database marketing responsibility. Of course, he may refuse to do so, in which case the risk is of losing power to database marketers!

Implications for a calling sales force

Sales staff are expensive, so we want every customer they visit to be a good quality prospect. We need them to structure their visits to customers as effectively as possible i.e. only when face to face presence is really needed to initiate or move the customer forward through the sales cycle.

Database marketing helps sales staff to call on more prospects who really do want to place large orders and less prospects who are just 'testing the water'. It also ensures that they spend less time looking for new business or servicing marginal accounts. It can provide information on existing accounts and on new customers. It should provide a strong framework for telemarketing to work closely with sales staff to deliver more business. The normal activity pattern of a calling sales force is not geared to frequent customer contact or many large orders. See Figure 18.1 for a typical activity analysis for a calling sales force.

A database marketing system can be used to measure and analyse sales results. It should be able to provide all the key sales productivity ratios, such as sales per call and calls per day. It should enable the relative productivity of sales staff to be assessed. It should also help sales staff plan their sales efforts, and may help with journey planning. The database can be used to create geographical 'clusters', so that the sales office can set appointments and work

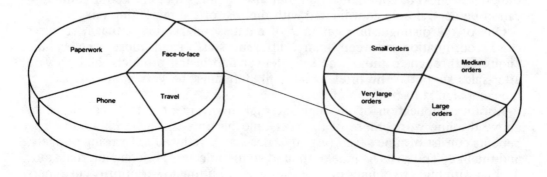

SALES TIME ANALYSIS   ORDER SIZE ANALYSIS

Figure 18.1: Sales time and revenue analysis

out sensible journey plans. It should monitor customer behaviour, such as buying cycles and order values, so sales staff can establish when customers are ready to buy, how often, and what sort of purchase levels they may reach.

A database marketing system achieves the above by:

- Gathering and processing leads, whether via direct mail, trade or national press advertising, telephone marketing, TV and radio, inserted or delivered leaflet, catalogues or exhibitions. These leads are delivered, prioritized, to sales staff, with the assurance that the customer was carefully targeted as being a good prospect, has responded to a campaign, and has already received further information on the product or service which is the subject of the lead.
- Rationalizing prospecting, enabling sales staff to spend more time converting prospects and developing more business with existing customers. This rationalization is a result of the more proactive marketing effort which database marketing encourages. It makes it easier to identify and reach opportunity markets and segments, ensuring that sales staff are used for the task for which they are most needed – making the most profitable sales.
- Gathering prospect data, enabling sales staff to plan their own sales efforts and prepare more thoroughly for their approach to the customer. The breadth and depth of customer information gives sales staff a deeper understanding of the customer and his needs, enabling them to tailor their proposals more effectively and to determine sales strategy more precisely – from which customer staff will be seen through to what needs to be discussed when they are seen.
- Getting information to customers, enabling them to move faster towards purchase, ensuring that sales staff are not just information providers.

- Identifying which prospects are 'hottest' and when they are likely to want to buy. This helps to schedule visits. It also means that customers who are serious will derive satisfaction from having their needs dealt with quickly. The system should ensure that sales staff know when the customer receives the information, preventing any waste of time before the call.
- Enabling further communications or actions to be triggered automatically (e.g. follow up sales or service activities), as part of the contact strategy.
- Sustaining customer loyalty, reducing the required frequency of 'maintenance' visits, and allowing sales staff to concentrate on moving forward sales cycles or resolving serious problems. Provided the communication is relevant, and not for its own sake, many customers prefer maintenance activity to be by mail. Campaign coordination ensures that customers receive a structured, non-overlapping flow of communication about products and services which meet their needs.

In exchange for these benefits, sales staff also have obligations. In many campaigns, they form the last link in the chain – the final element of the contact strategy which delivers the business. This does not mean that they have to follow up every lead that arrives. Some leads will be low priority. Others may arrive at a difficult time, when existing customers are crying out for attention. But sales staff must give leads due attention. When a high priority lead arrives, it means that a customer has expressed a need and is expecting to hear from the salesperson.

Sales staff are also a vital link in the flow of information. The system depends on their feedback. If the system is not told the result of sales activities, it will be much less useful in determining the optimum strategy for managing customers. The feedback channels provided must be used. Even if the eventual results are picked up through order entry systems and the like, these are unlikely to operate quickly enough or provide all the required marketing information. The better the quality of input to these databases, the better the campaigns and the better the leads. No salesperson should be a market researcher, but the system should provide a streamlined framework to encourage sales staff to help maintain database quality.

The sales office

Many sales forces are supported by a sales office, which may also act as a telesales centre and perhaps also take on service functions. Many staff working in a sales office without a database marketing system are normally carrying out one or two basic database marketing tasks, such as response handling – dealing with inbound enquiries, or fulfilment – ensuring that the customer gets what he wants (e.g. a product brochure, confirmation of order entry, delivery or installation). Many such staff feel they have enough work just dealing with the existing volume of enquiries coming in. Some staff spend more time on the beginning of the sales cycle, identifying prospects or discovering their needs, and on more profitable ends to the sales cycle, taking more and larger orders. Staff already in telemarketing units or with a telemarketing role in a sales office will be working on outbound direct marketing. The introduction of full database marketing helps such staff to achieve large scale improvements in their effectiveness, by:

- Providing improved marketing databases for identifying the best prospects for particular services and products. This means that the leads coming to sales offices will be higher quality and that better prospects will be identified for telemarketing campaigns.
- Getting leads to sales offices more quickly, ensuring that they are fresh. This means that the customer is more likely to commit to the next stage of the sales cycle and less likely to have pursued enquiries with competitive suppliers.
- Prioritizing the leads it delivers. This ensures that sales staff know which leads to give attention to first.
- Making sure, through the careful targeting of campaigns and copy design, that leads are high quality.
- Providing a mechanism for actioning and following up leads derived from telemarketing campaigns more quickly and effectively.
- In some cases, automatically sending customers the information they need. This enables office sales staff to concentrate on scheduling sales appointments with the right customers and on closing orders. It also enables telemarketing staff to concentrate on moving the customer to the next stage in the sales cycle rather than providing information.
- Ensuring that the leads received contain more relevant information than before, giving staff a flying start in moving to the next stage in the sales cycle.
- Improving the basis for monitoring the sales cycle by providing better reports on open orders, etc.
- Facilitating coordination of local sales office efforts with those of other marketing functions – sales staff, other channels, telemarketing, etc., as part of a coherent contact strategy.

In a business where coverage of many small to medium size customers (business or consumer) is important, where potential sales do not justify a calling sales force, but do justify a more proactive marketing stance than setting up a retail outlet and relying on customers to call, adopting a database marketing approach enables the sales office to serve as a remote account management office, deploying a combination of mail and telephone. The most important asset which enables this approach to be taken is information on the database which indicates customer potential in terms of what, how much, how frequently and when they buy, and details of how to contact them.

The telemarketing operation

If a local telemarketing operation is established, it can use workstations on-line to the customer database to:

- Handle data entry
- Automatically dial and present the next call from the list, rejecting engaged and unanswered lines and routing answered call to the appropriate available representative
- Distribute inbound calls to available representatives
- Manage call scheduling.

This automated approach greatly improves the effectiveness of local telemarketing functions and helps minimize backlogs. The quality of the information used by telemarketing functions will be improved by better targeting and data output facilities, which should provide high quality lists for the telemarketing function, including contact histories. These lists should be formatted so as to be immediately and easily usable by the telemarketing representative. The quality of information coming in from telemarketing campaigns is improved by automated scripting and on-screen entry of responses. Paper handling should be minimized.

Such an operation can support the full range of telemarketing tasks – order taking, appointment making, prospecting, qualifying, research and so forth. It can also provide a customer care or account management function, allowing many different ways of increasing sales potential:

- More frequent contacts – particularly important for small businesses and certain consumer customers. Without this, there is greater risk of switching to competition.
- A greater variety of customer contacts – beyond those made in the course of selling. For example, customer needs may be ascertained in more depth and attitudes identified. New contacts within existing accounts can be made.
- More carefully designed customer contact, through planned customer care campaigns with tight scripting, with representatives having access to accurate, complete customer data.
- The development of defined plans for each customer. Access to the data and use of scoring routines ensures that contacts are coordinated and timed to suit the customer's buying cycle. The representative will also be able to show good knowledge of the customer's situation.

19 Distribution channels

Distribution channel policy can be one of the main stumbling blocks to the adoption or successful implementation of database marketing. This is often because some of the fundamental concepts of distribution channel strategy and database marketing are not understood.

The term 'distribution channel' is used widely in marketing analysis. The very name implies goods or services coming from a central point and being scattered outwards or downwards. As most suppliers of products or services who use third party channels have discovered, successful channel management requires much more than the ability to 'pipeline' products or services to the customer. A good distribution channel is a relationship channel, the relationships being both with the channel members (those who own and/or work in the channel organizations) and with the customers who use the channel to conduct their relationship with the supplier. In analysing the nature of a company's relationship with its customers, particularly as expressed through its distribution channels, we need to specify the relationship's functions:

- A vehicle for communications dialogue. From customers comes communication about needs, behaviour and a variety of other information (business, personal, etc.) which helps the supplier (including any third party distributor) satisfy the needs of customers better (including their need for communication). From suppliers comes communication about satisfying customer needs: products and services and how they provide (different) benefits to different types of customer; image-related communication e.g. describing the supplier and what he is doing to meet customer needs; transmission of company and service branding information; information helping the customer access the supplier and obtain the right products and services; information providing reassurance and so forth. The information may be communicated in a variety of ways: letters, telephone calls, sales visits, visits to a retail location, on bills, on packaging, in discussions with management.

- Pre- and post-sales support. These are important functions in many industrial and some consumer markets. Pre-sales support is closely related to after-sales support. It often includes consultancy and diagnostic work and other elements of what is sometimes called sales service (but not those relating to availability of stock). In some cases, it is impossible to distinguish after-sales support on one product from pre-sales support on another, for a given customer, while some advisory work may flow through from before the sale to after the sale.
- Commercial distribution – the passing of title, ownership or right to use a product or service and the collection of payment from the customer. Physical distribution is ensuring that the product or service is actually available to and usable by the customer. This includes ensuring equipment or service availability and supply, holding inventory, installation and commissioning.
- A vehicle for a relationship. The above functions of a relationship channel are rather technical. We must not forget that there is a strong psychological function over and above these functions – the embodiment or the symbol of the overall relationship. For example, image studies on many industrial sales forces show that one of the main determinants of a company's image is its sales and service staff. The same applies to the lay-out and staff behaviour in a retail outlet.

Does the customer choose the channel?

Before discussing the relationship between database marketing and distribution channels, we need to understand how channels are developed and managed. There are two broad views on channel choice and management: customer driven and supplier driven.

Under the customer-driven approach, customers are held to choose the channel through which to acquire or use a product or service. They use two sets of criteria, one set relating to their perceptions of each channel's performance on important factors. Included here are factors such as product or service supply (quality, availability, ability to customize, etc.), price and terms (and other costs of doing business – especially those borne by the customer), image and branding, convenience or location, type and quality of sales service (including ease of use of the channel), type and quality of trust in the relationship, and professionalism in the sales approach. The customer's perceptions of these factors are affected not only by the channel's actual performance, but also by e.g. word of mouth recommendations, marketing communications, specific experiences of transactions with the channel. The other set of factors relates to the customer's needs in relation to the above – i.e. what benefits he is seeking in his relationship with the channel.

If this customer driven view is correct, then channels would evolve to meet customers' needs and work hard to create favourable perceptions. Note that customers' needs and perceptions are not static. Customers enter and leave the markets which channels serve. They extend or contract their needs. Product ranges expand and contract, and prices rise and fall. New applications are developed for existing products. Channel capacities and resources evolve, often under the influence of competition. The result is that channels are continually under pressure to change to meet market needs. If we accept this view, we can understand why customers may choose a number of different channels through which to acquire a given product or service.

Although a supplier with a monopoly or a very strong brand can restrict the supply of his product to specific channels and still achieve his market share objectives, in general this view holds that market share objectives will usually force a supplier to find ways of using whatever channels command the market coverage to deliver his market share objectives.

On this view, the reason why different channels exist is that they deliver different sets of benefits to customers – but customers require different sets of benefits at different times, which is why we find it difficult to 'tell' customers 'Always go to channel X' (e.g. small customers should always buy through telemarketing). If a small customer wants to see a salesperson from us, then we may have to resort to pricing to ensure that the visit is economic (e.g. by not extending a 'direct order discount' to him), rather than telling him we cannot see him, or make a salesperson available cheaply. However, no supplier can ensure that every sales visit is profitable, any more than a credit card company can ensure that every transaction is profitable to it. We are in the business of averages here. Most companies handle this by marketing rather than pricing. They identify likely potential (not just first sale, but lifetime) of the customer, and refer him to the appropriate channel with all its benefits. But if this fails, they deal with him through a non-optimum channel, as effectively as possible. This implies a significant role for database marketing contact strategy as an economic manager of the customer channel relationship, as contact strategies can be adjusted according to data gathered as part of the dialogue.

The supplier-driven approach holds that suppliers choose which channel to access their customers by, according to relative costs, administrative convenience, market coverage, strategic positioning of the brand, precedent (inertia of customers, the competition or the supplier himself), and degree of monopoly (on supplier or channel side). Therefore, channels must adapt to meet supplier needs. In certain markets (e.g. the motor market), where each brand is carefully controlled and products are significantly differentiated by design, performance and promotion, leading suppliers are able to call the shots. The question is whether a company's brand is strong enough to appeal to customers without the support of total channel branding. Making a brand available through multiple channels and sustaining its presence is the ultimate marketing test of this.

In practice, most markets have examples of both customer driven and supplier driven channels, and most companies control some of their channels more than others. Factors which determine this include:

- Frequency and type of contact – if a customer requires frequent or extensive contact before, during or after the sale, and if the likely value of the relationship (not just the individual sale) is high, then a direct sales force can be deployed more economically (but see comment on solutions below). If the likely value of the relationship is low, the contact strategy of the supplier may be limited to reference to another channel, or to a short sales visit followed by fulfilment by other means.
- Productivity and effectiveness – cost factors are dealt with above. Effectiveness refers to whether the channel can actually fulfil the task.
- Organizational implications – although it may be optimal (from the customer's point of view or given the economics of a situation) to use a particular channel, a supplier may be 'constitutionally incapable' of using it, because it is found difficult to manage. Companies which in the past have used only a direct sales force often have severe problems in managing a dealer channel, not because of channel conflict, but because they do not know how to do business with dealers.
- Data and control implications – a supplier may feel unhappy about making his products available through third parties, because he feels he cannot or does not know how to market in this way (control his brand, obtain market data, etc.).

Branding the relationship

The best way to manage channels so as to provide the right portfolio of contact strategy options lies in the area of channel relationship branding. This means understanding the relationship between the customer and each channel, how it is expressed through the branding of the channel and working to develop that relationship so as to assist the achievement of marketing objectives and to meet customer needs even more.

Once this approach is adopted, a company can decide how to influence customers to choose between channels, according to their needs and those of the company. It should aim to help customers access it through channels which most suit their needs. 'Channel portfolio marketing' might be a better term, as it conveys the idea of offering a portfolio of channels to customers, each with distinctive benefits and branding and as part of carefully defined contact strategies. The marketing database plays an important role in establishing customer needs (in response handling and in relationship management). The database marketing system can then recommend appropriate channels (through contact strategy), at the level of the individual customer and for entire market sectors.

If this approach is taken, database marketing will not be a threat to existing channels (unless they act as a significant constraint to customer choice of how the relationship should be conducted). Instead, it will be seen as an important element of the process of attuning channels to customer needs.

Conclusion: Making it happen

The four main elements required to make database marketing happen are:

1. Corporate refocusing (creating a customer-led approach to doing business)
2. Capability (data, systems, staff, supplier and business partner) development
3. Marketing applications development
4. Policy development

Corporate refocusing

A new approach to marketing and business can be created through the introduction of a very strong customer focus and orientation, supported by the computerization of customer data and other marketing information, of marketing communication campaigns and of business management in general. This new approach is then overlaid on (not confronted with) a company's existing approach, so that the latter begins to change.

The essence of the approach is looking to the future, creating a vision of how the business will develop by getting closer to its customers and sustaining a strong and mutually valuable relationship with them, identifying what new revenue streams can be created and what heavy costs can be avoided, and capturing these opportunities by innovative marketing approaches.

Creating this refocusing in a large company usually involves a long campaign, with presentation after presentation required to educate senior managers and convince them of the benefits of database marketing and the need to make the necessary substantial systems and human investment.

Capability development

Development of the basic capability or infrastructure can permit the introduction of innovative and cost reducing marketing programmes to a company. Without this infrastructure, a company would find it extremely difficult to mount effective campaigns. The main elements of capability development are as follows:

Database development

A database of customers, prospects and business partners can be constructed. The database contains fundamental data about each person or company, and additional data relating to their transactions with the company (purchases, credit taken, visits to exhibitions, etc.). These data provide the information needed to target and attract new customers, profitably meet more of the needs of existing customers, and identify new, lower cost ways of reaching and selling to customers.

Marketing system development

Computer systems can be developed to hold, manage, enhance and manipulate the data, so that they can be used as described above. It also includes application sub-systems to support specific applications, such as telemarketing, mail order, credit cards, accumulation of promotional credits, lead generation for the sales force or dealers, exhibition invitations, insurance and pensions schemes, and club or user group marketing.

Staff development

Staff skills can be developed so that a company can deploy the data and system to its marketing advantage. Without these skills, even the best database marketing system will not work. Often, these skills are acquired on a temporary basis at first, from consultancies and service agencies, but they must be brought in-house eventually.

Supplier development

Links can be forged with a variety of suppliers who can carry out the following functions: data provision, management and interpretation; marketing systems management; marketing application development; creative marketing services. They need to understand the company and its needs. A relationship of trust must also be built, as database marketing may eventually drive all the company's marketing strategy.

Business partner development

Partnerships can be created with other companies who benefit from one or other strand of the company's strategy. They include companies involved in joint promotions to the customers on the company's database and in distributing the company's products.

Business partner development is essential to the implementation of the database marketing approach. Once we have identified the potential represented by our customer base, our prime asset, we usually need the help of other companies in exploiting this potential. For example, a traditional manufacturing company or a retailer may need the help of an established general merchandise mail order supplier in broadening its relationship with customers.

All the above developments should result in a marketing capability distinguished for its ability to develop and implement new strategic directions, its comprehensiveness, its competitiveness and its ability to meet customer needs quickly and suitably.

Marketing applications development

Marketing applications development covers the development of approaches to marketing which use the newly created capability, i.e. ways in which the new capability will be applied. These applications are not individual policies, which can be initiated and terminated at short notice. They represent fundamental commitments to a changed way of doing business with customers and business partners. Examples of marketing applications development include:

- Consumer and business promotion
- Targeted mailing, mail order and fulfilment facility
- Credit card management
- Financial services marketing
- Targeted branding
- Telemarketing systems
- Dealer, distributor or agent management systems
- Club and user group marketing support
- Low cost distribution support
- Data marketing.

Policy development

Policy development is distinguished from the last element by focus on specific shorter term objectives. Policies are defined in terms of one or more particular campaigns (e.g. launch of a specific new life insurance policy, a customer loyalty questionnaire campaign), usually relying heavily on one or more of the capabilities and applications mentioned above.

For most users of database marketing, much of this work is delegated (at least partly) to direct marketing agencies. However, the planning of the coordinated series of campaigns which make up the policy must remain the responsibility of the company. If this planning and coordination does not take place in-house, database marketing activity may become divorced from the mainstream of company business.

Conclusions

We have seen that database marketing can affect every aspect of marketing strategy and implementation, though we feel we have barely skimmed the surface. Our feelings are partly prompted by the fact that every day we learn something new, either through work we are doing with our clients, or through hearing about a new development in technology or practice elsewhere.

Despite all this, the messages of database marketing are ancient marketing messages:

- Know who your customers are
- Keep in touch with them
- Allow them to speak to you when they want to
- Give them good reasons (benefits) for maintaining their relationship with you
- Do all this carefully (in a well-planned and steadily implemented manner)
- Do it cost-effectively.

Index